Tokyo Void

jovis

TOKYO

VOID

Possibilities in Absence

Marieluise Jonas / Heike Rahmann

jovis

Cover Image: Tokyo Skyline, Marieluise Jonas
Images used by permission:
p. 52 Toshiyuki Makizumi
p. 139 Hajime Ishikawa

Book design, drawings, and photographs: Marieluise Jonas, Heike Rahmann
Lithography: f1bild, Berlin
Printing and binding: GRASPO CZ, a.s., Zlín

Bibliographic information published by the Deutsche Nationalbibliothek
The Deutsche Nationalbibliothek lists this publication in the Deutsche Nationalbibliografie; detailed bibliographic data are available on the Internet at http://dnb.d-nb.de

jovis Verlag GmbH
Kurfürstenstraße 15/16
10785 Berlin

www.jovis.de

jovis books are available worldwide in selected bookstores. Please contact your nearest bookseller or visit www.jovis.de for information concerning your local distribution.

ISBN 978-3-86859-272-6

Contents

Roppongi, Minato-ku, Central Tokyo
Tokyo Tower and neighborhood viewed from Roppongi Hills Observatory, 2008

PREFACE

In 1996, the Japanese photographer Masataka Nakano published a collection of images of Tokyo in his book *Tokyo Nobody*. His book instantaneously sparked an interest in everyone who thought they knew what this city was like: a busy, restless place that never sleeps. But through his work, Nakano cleverly challenges our collective understanding of the city. Each photograph depicts a scene from Tokyo's urban landscape that all of us immediately recognize: a chaotic collection of miniature and tall buildings; landmarks such as the Tokyo Tower; advertising billboards; the metropolitan expressway; and meticulously manicured vegetation. The views seem randomly selected and could be taken anywhere in the city: a depiction of the everyday. Yet, what seems so profoundly familiar at first sight carries at the second glance some strangeness, as the images lack any trace of human presence. Thus, Nakano looks at the familiar but is still able to present a view that contradicts common readings of the city.

Tokyo Void is about the urban landscape of the city. It combines two seemingly contrasting entities: Tokyo, the largest city in the world, on the one hand; and void and vacancy, on the other hand.

Nishi-Shinjuku, Shinjuku-ku
Areas of low-rise neighborhoods, enclosed by high-rise buildings
View to the West from Tokyo Metropolitan Government Building, Winter 2007

Similar to Nakano's images, *Tokyo Void* plays with the notion of contrasting views. Through the lens of vacancy, it explores new layers and deeper readings of a city that is rooted in history and caught in superlatives. No news broadcast or documentary without the hustling crowds of Shibuya crossing, Shinjuku's neon lights, zooming Shinkansen trains, or the flurry of the TOPIX. Tokyo is presented as the vast and surreal place from the future. A city of immediate simultaneousness, "near-ness" and "now-ness,"[1] a conglomeration of profanity, the proverbial city of concrete and chaos, *Blade Runner* and Metabolism. Tokyo's image as an exotic dream destination is (in) famously manifested in the name of the German pop-music band Tokio Hotel, who saw their dream of staying in a Tokyo Hotel as nonachievable.

While there is certainly some truth to the images presented—as there is in any stereotypical framing—it only symbolizes how Tokyo remains stuck in the well-known, the exhausted, and the stereotypes. *Tokyo Void* invites questioning of the city's superficial image by looking inward. It provokes discovering the detail, the small and overlooked, the quiet and surprising. In other words: to see Tokyo from the inside, through possibilities in absence presented by urban voids. We consider urban voids as a groundscape for dynamic urban ecology. Voids are constituted by different types of vacant spaces and processes of development ranging from small and disjointed leftover spaces, gaps between buildings—which Suzuki describes as "linear auras"—to spatial by-products of elevated expressways and train lines.[2] This image of the city presented by urban voids is closer to the everyday, but remains largely absent from contemporary discussions, reflections, and representations of the city. In foregrounding the urban vacant land, its morphology, meanings, uses, materiality, and performance, we set up a landscape approach to understanding Tokyo. "Landscape," as Mathur and da Cunha state, "plays a fundamental role" in the reading of the built environment.[3] It "creates not only the ground for inhabitation, but also the subjects of knowledge and the practices of everyday life; it provides the vocabulary of the land."[4] Voids, as part of the landscape, can provide us with a perspective through which we see the city: the multiple scales between the detail and the overall; the processes of emergence and decline; multiple timescales; the cultural and policy frameworks that inform the perceptions and occupations of Tokyo's vacant land.

Since the concept of vacant space emerged in writings as an opportunity for urban activation, authors have favored the strong romantic notion of the interstitial, the vague, and the otherness. So at the beginning of this project, it was only too easy to follow that thread. On our first encounter with Tokyo, dating back to 2001 when we worked as landscape architecture interns for the renowned Japanese architect Kisho Kurokawa, the discovery of ubiquitous plots of vacant land immediately attracted our attention. In light of Tokyo's specific urban conditions—such as extreme density, scarcity of space, rapid transformation, and urban growth—which we explored during our extended stay, the question appeared as to why these spaces were not used or even considered for alternative activities. In what we now understand as an implicitly European view of Tokyo's small voids, we started an investigation into potential utilization strategies for vacant spaces. An early approach included designing a series of vacant spaces adjacent to the Tokyo Metropolitan expressway in Setagaya ward to make these sites accessible to the public. Since then, we have explored other appropriation strategies, such as on-site interventions and installations, and have tested their interrelation with various forms of ownership, levels of engagement, and responsibilities.

But the Japanese context provides us with other challenges, and too many important questions remained unanswered. Through our numerous site visits and discussions with our Japanese colleagues, it was evident that it was necessary take a step back. Before we were able to speculate further about activation strategies, we had to really dig into the phenomenon of vacant space in the context of Japan in general, and Tokyo in particular. One of the key ambitions of the book is to ascertain the distinct qualities and typologies of Tokyo's temporary vacant spaces, while considering the distinct morphological and temporal qualities of the temporary vacant urban spaces in development and design. Understanding what functions urban voids possess is vital to their activation. While we certainly attempt to "introduce to the West the beautiful products of the Japanese mind,"[5] we will also raise some critical issues necessary to contextualize and reevaluate the potentials for activating void spaces, both in Tokyo as well as in other cities. As such, we hope to provide a fresh view to readers both familiar and unfamiliar with the topic and the city. For readers familiar with the situation of vacancy in other cultural contexts, we aim to provide an extended perspective on the discourse by introducing a new contextual situation. For readers, familiar with Tokyo, we hope to open a new way of exploring the richness of the city and unfamiliar concepts, while also stimulating discussion about alternative practices of urban transformation and regeneration. As we hope to demonstrate through this book, voids and Tokyo are not mutually exclusive entities. And the journey of alternative practices has just begun.

This book would not have been possible without the tremendous support provided by following people and institutions.

We deeply indebted to Dr. Hiroshi Ota and his Lab of Sustainable Urban Regeneration at the Institute of Industrial Science at the University of Tokyo, for his continuous support during the duration of the project and for stimulating discussions that enriched our exploration into urban regeneration in Japan.

Special thanks go to Dr. Maria Rita Dionisio and Dr. Maria Claudia De Souza who assisted us in any possible way in organizing resources, infrastructure, and most importantly access to relevant data.

We are grateful to the Institute of Industrial Science for their generous support through our Visiting Research Fellowship, and for hosting us and our students during our numerous visits to Tokyo. RMIT University provided us with an Architecture and Design School Research Fund to support our fieldwork in Japan.

We thank Erik Johansson for his fantastic technical assistance in setting up of one of our interventions. Thanks also to Assistant Professor Christian Dimmer of the Department of Urban Engineering, University of Tokyo, and Dr. Jared Braiterman for valuable discussions and sharing their insight into public and green spaces in Tokyo.

Our gratitude goes out to Toshiyuki Makizumi and Yoshiko Yanai for developing such a fantastic project like Ondi, and for kindly offering us to participate in events and to use the site for a design studio with our students. Through their enthusiasm and generous hospitality, they are an inspiration to us in seeing the beautiful qualities of Japanese space.

And finally to all Tokyoites whom we met during our explorations and who were supportive of two foreigners strolling and photographing their intimate neighborhoods in search of vacant spaces.

Neighborhood in Bunkyo-ku, Center North-East Tokyo
Photo taken from Bunkyo Civic Center 2007

INTRODUCTION

Voids in Density

I believe that any place has the potential to become the center of the world.

Hiroshi Naito

Ruptures in the surface are abundant in any city where processes of growth, restructuring, or decline produce urban voids: spaces in transition from one stage of development to another. Voids can be understood as ground or basic canvas on which other actions play out. They are a metaphor for the interrupted and brutally exposed land where remnants of lives are scattered, shattered, forgotten, hidden, and revived. Over the past two decades, these spaces have regained global attention across a wide range of audience including academia, design practice, and the general society who discovered vacancy as opportunity for creative and ecological urbanism.

Urban voids also are examples for the ever-changing city and a potential urban wilderness. They are not just mere gaps in the urban landscape, but also leftover buffer zones without clearly defined functions or boundaries. Their form and location, often distant or unsuitable for development, leave these places outside of any consideration for formal uses. Used as garbage dumps and other undesirable or illicit activities, these leftover spaces are viewed unsafe and are neglected by most.

Yet, the notion of unformulated existence that attracts the unwanted can also be viewed as indicator for a potential counter perspective on systematic, clean, efficient, and productive urban space.

> The forest that at one time surrounded cities and villages, where bears and wolves, but also the nightmares would hide, where the fantasies and the very idea of liberty itself were shoved far from the city, put into the corners, restricted and in an unbelievable act of clemency, protected. And here it is now that that same forest rises again, exactly there in the cities where the territory's systems of appropriation and control are most ancient and crumbling.[1]

The metaphor of the forest captures the quality of voids, which are seemingly formed through cracks in the urban surface: unplanned vegetated remnants that grow and develop habitats as an urban wilderness, the built city's negative, the interstitial and the marginal, spaces abandoned or in the process of transformation. The urban wilderness becomes a place for cohabitation of humans and other nonhuman species. Vegetative successions of plants, an unplanned and unpredictable wilderness on small scale, form a potentially dangerous field of the other, yet offer possibility for discovery and escapes from the known. Voids speak to a transient ideal of imperfection—a principle of aesthetic appreciation in longing for authenticity. The idea of imperfection nourishes the thought that nothing is finished, all is ephemeral and fading—and in fading, the most beautiful. Transient spaces serve no productive purpose. They offer ground for juxtaposition, unintended discoveries and nonproductive activities, experiences, which are unplanned and momentary. They offer just a glimpse of the accidental, the unfinished and may heal the hurting and bleak emptiness of the indifferent state of void.

Tokyo's Voids

In the complex, multilayered urban environment of Tokyo, voids are inconspicuous, subtle breaks in a continuous urban tissue. Of the overall land area in Tokyo, 4 percent is classified as unused land. In Japan, the cultural codex describes a strong respect for private property. Often, only minimal or subtle markers are required to identify boundaries between private and public. A very common inventory of the vacant spaces is a tiny, almost invisible rope that separates a site from the surrounding context. From a Western perspective, it raises the question of what in fact is to be protected: the site from the potential intruder, or the potential intruder from the unpredictability of the site. Its physical presence may be weak, but in Tokyo—one of the safest cities in the world—the symbolic meaning is strong enough to prevent entry and unappreciated activities. In other places, the vacant sites are well hidden away from human interaction behind tall fences and walls, allowing plants the rare opportunity to reappropriate the urban landscape.

The density and extreme vastness of the metropolis stands in stark contrast to the smallness of most voids. In Tokyo, the traditional identification of urban space by status—legal, economical, and functional—is challenged by a complex ambiguity of a very effective use of scarce spatial recourses through overlays and interweaving structures. Land is used incredibly efficiently. Infrastructures permeate all layers of the city where multistory metropolitan expressways hover above rivers, netted golf courses sit on top of shopping complexes, and roads tunnel under cemeteries.[2] Atelier Bow-Wow defines the "impossible" architectures of Tokyo as "Pet Architecture,"[3] and likens their character—their cuteness as small companions in the city—to pets. These "pets" often have irregular plots and are extremely small, while the average plot size of private dwellings in Tokyo is approximately 150 square meters for a single dwelling. Even plots as tiny as thirty square meters are recognized as suitable for dwellings and setback rules only apply to the street frontage, so that land can effectively be built up to 100 percent.

The presence of urban voids adds to the strangeness and chaos of Tokyo's urban landscape—as vacancy eventually does in any city—but in the context of extreme density and effective use and occupation of spatial recourses, they can also be seen as a calming entity. In fact, these empty spaces offer rare atmospheric qualities. While 4 percent vacant space is not much in a global context, voids in Tokyo are truly an incredible spatial resource in a city, which despite all efforts, still significantly lacks open space. Only 6 percent of Tokyo's urban area is classified as open space, which includes parks, gardens, and plazas.[4] This translates into a mere three square meters of open space per capita. By comparison, residents in Berlin have access to thirty-seven square meters per person,[5] while New York offers twenty-seven square meters per person.[6] Public space in Tokyo is not only limited in size, but often also in design and accessibility. Many public parks are of very poor quality consisting only of small graveled surface squares, sparse vegetation, and the obligatory play equipment. Green spaces and parks that offer a better design and recreational quality are regulated by opening hours, and permitted activities are heavily restricted. Shinjuku Gyoen, one of the largest parks in the city center, has an entry fee of 400 yen (roughly $US4.00) and closes its gate around 4 PM, without any significant adjustment of the closing hours throughout seasons. Therefore, most of the three million daily commuters in Shinjuku station—the biggest station in Tokyo—cannot use the park after work, although the beautifully managed park is just a short five-minute walk from the station.

These public green spaces are not only spatially disconnected from the everyday urban environment. Hiroshi Ota, founding member of Tokyo Picnic Club (TPC), even goes so far as to describe parks as alien places to Tokyo's residents: "If anyone invites his friend to go to the park, it will be regarded as a sign that he should have very serious confessions, or he should want to try the duel. Parks are quite disconnected from public lives in Tokyo."[7]

Scale study: Zooming in on a vacant site in Yanaka, Taito-ku, North-West Tokyo
Google Earth images

These aspects of regulation, inaccessibility, and disconnectedness of open green space raise further questions on the value of the already limited open space. The Tokyo-based design anthropologist Jared Braiterman brings the common perception of Tokyo's green space to the point: "When I explain that Hitachi Ltd. and the U.S. Council on Foreign Relations awarded me a fellowship to research and write about Tokyo green space, many Japanese colleagues look perplexed. Wouldn't Paris or Washington, D.C. be a better place? The assumption is that cities with better urban planning begun in the 19th century offer a superior urban atmosphere."[8]

But these issues and perceptions do not mean that there is no need for public space in Tokyo. In fact, it suggests that the current formal practices of open space design do not necessarily meet the demands and expectations of the citizens. Tokyo not only has a great array of alternative green spaces as expressed in the numerous—often quite opulent—flowerpot gardens, but also a number of beautiful interventions take place in which residents start to shape their own city. Similar to landscape architect Hajime Ishikawa, who ventures through the city to map Tokyo's other landscape,[9] Braiterman uses his blog "Tokyo Green Space" to discuss and promote these smaller, hidden traces of a greener Tokyo. Alternative spatial practices are slowly emerging in Tokyo.

Global Practice

However, in many places around the world, people, planners, designers, and local governments have already started to embrace voids as a valid opportunity for urban regeneration. The popularity and growing interest in the topic is also reflected in the large number of publications that have emerged since the mid-nineteen-nineties with a focus on urban interstitial spaces, terrain vague, and temporary urbanism. The writings cover a wide range of contexts and issues that can be grouped into three trajectories: first, the phenomenological nature of voids; second, economic processes leading to vacancy; and third, new programs and uses for vacant spaces.

Phenomenological readings of vacant sites are largely influenced by the writing of Catalan urbanist Ignasi De Sola-Morales. In his famous 1995 essay "Terrains Vagues", he began to frame the visual and aesthetic qualities of these "strange and undefined empty city spaces" from the perspective of photography.[10] He writes that these "Unincorporated margins, interior islands void of activity, oversights, these areas are simply un-inhabited, un-safe, un-productive."[11] In critiquing the homogeneity of contemporary architecture and urban design, he suggests that these qualities "foreign to the urban system" also provide opportunity of alternative appropriation. Cassegard summarizes this capacity of urban voids in pragmatic terms. He argues, "What's so good with a wasteland is precisely that they're unregulated and neglected by the authorities, thus creating a breathing space where users themselves can reshape space according to their needs, desires and whims."[12]

The second thematic examines the phenomena of social, political, and economic conditions that inform both urban transformation processes in general, and the production of vacant space in particular. ***Shrinking Cities,*** first discussed by Philip Oswalt in 2005, framed urban voids in the context of urban and economic decline.[13] Further, suburbanization processes, the decline of heavy industry, but also political regime change migration processes initiated social exodus, which has produced perforated and fragmented cities across Europe and Northern America. Concepts of waste and wasting of spatial recourses are reccurring issues that govern the discourse as illustrated in Alan Berger's ***Drosscape.***[14]

Possibly the most widely recognized discussion on urban voids focuses on temporary uses. Here, voids function as icons to reappropriate the city and to deny consumerism and a bourgeois public. Examples include urban subcultures that reclaim abandoned space for community gardens, adventure playgrounds, or urban farming. These informal uses have led to questioning of established ideas about urban planning. By the beginning of 2000, numerous scholars had started to describe the catalytic effects of these appropriation processes on urban development and regeneration in the European context.[15] The focus here shifted to the spatial capacities of urban voids and provided a detailed understanding of the involved processes for activation that could be utilized to ***catalyze*** urban regeneration and to "pioneer dynamic master planning."[16] In the last few years, new interpretations of abandoned spaces have emerged. These writings began to foreground the reading of urban voids as a materialscape, where remnant vegetation and unsealed surfaces not only inspire creative human inhabitation, but also contribute to the larger urban ecology.[17]

Most of these case studies and theories remain centered in the European and North American contexts and the particular concerns of urban decline. But how valid are these concepts in Tokyo and another cultural context? It seems that the phenomenological reading of voids as *Other,* the idea of ***strangeness*** as defined by De Solà-Morales is quickly exhausted in Tokyo—the place of proverbial incongruity. While some of the vague spaces might be linked to mechanisms of reconstruction and developments, others exist only ***because*** of Tokyo and its particular patterns and logic.

This raises the question of what we can gain by investigating the specific processes that shape these spaces in Tokyo. How do familiar questions change in an unfamiliar context? We argue that by expanding the view beyond the Western notion of vacancy and spatial productions, the vocabulary of urban voids will change and grow. By looking at a place that is highly driven by efficiency, we can explore other performative aspects of voids that add value to the urban life. And we will see a typology, morphology, and use of voids that is tightly connected to the spatial conditions and cultural practices in this city.

Urban Void, Yanaka, Taito-ku
Vacant plots replace buildings.

Cultural Aspects of Void

Working in a Japanese context, urban voids reflect the socioeconomic and cultural conditions and processes of urban development under which they have formed, as they would in any other context. However, the specific philosophical and cultural positions—where emptiness is seen as latent possibility, imperfection an ideal, and inwardness a spatial concept—can add to the repertoire of how urban voids are seen, and question established ideas.

The notion of void evokes very distinct reactions in a Japanese context, where ideas of *Mu* (the void) are deeply embedded in philosophical, religious, and spatial concepts, and can be found in Japanese terms such as *Ma* (in-between space, emptiness), *Wabi-Sabi* (imperfection), *Oku* (inwardness), or *Harappa* (open field, wild field).

The latter immediately evokes familiarity in Japanese urban voids. It defines urban voids distinctly as fantasy play spaces, playgrounds for exploration and games, and is widely used to refer to childhood memories of overgrown, open, vacant spaces conquered for play and adventure. As such, harappa seems to function as a code for instantly grasping the capacity the spaces offer, as Jun Aoki declares: "The wilderness is not fun in itself. Almost daily, one has to invent new ways of playing."[18]

Emptiness is traditionally perceived as an expression of latent possibility. Kenya Hara, designer and art director for Muji states: "Emptiness does not merely imply simplicity of form, logical sophistication, and the like. Rather, emptiness provides a space within which our imaginations can run free, vastly enriching our powers of perception and our mutual comprehension."[19] We like to think that these powers can extend to physical and metaphysical formless atmospheres.

The spatial concept oku, the innermost, describes a portion of a finite space, designed and staged to suggest infinity. How can this conceptual understanding of infinite internalization inform and guide the way we see urban voids? Oku yields the understanding of urban voids as inwardly oriented and deeply detailed spaces, rather than interchangeable volumes. In considering this quasi-infinite capacity, these spaces offer a possibility to trace an inwardly oriented nature of Tokyo.

Wabi-sabi, as a transient ideal of imperfection, remains a main principle of aesthetic appreciation in contemporary Japan. In this, the idea of the imperfect instills the thought that nothing is finished, all is ephemeral and fading—and in fading, the most beautiful. The cherry blossom is often cited as the clearest example: its fragile and ephemeral beauty is considered to be at its peak in the moment when the flower petals fall from the tree to drift in the wind. Yoshida Kenkō, Buddhist monk and author of the *Tsurezuregusa,* beautifully frames the deeply rooted cultural appreciation.

Tokyo—Micro scale of an urban giant

Video still "Gokiburi cam," spatial experiment by authors, 2010
The perspective of a cockroach extends the space of a small void to form a vast landscape.

In these essays, first printed in 1331, Kenkō contemplates, "In everything, no matter what it may be, uniformity is undesirable. Leaving something incomplete makes it interesting, and gives one the feeling that there is room for growth."[20] Can this powerful ideal of imperfection affect the way transient spaces are understood? Would this view enable the appreciation of beauty in the unfinished and ever-changing city, in its gaps and holes that have no function or purpose other than the silent waiting for development behind fences and immaculate white walls? Or would it lead to a less romantic but more realistic exclusion of the *other* in a society that strives for a community ideal of homogeneity?

We have structured the explorations of *Tokyo Void* in two parts. Part One focuses on the opportunities we see in voids through their performative quality both as places for inhabitation and transgression, as well as places for subtle ecologies. In Chapter One, we discuss strategies and tactics for spatial appropriation and formal design practices. We discover a "deep, quiet, comforting" organism, where "something human, something gloriously ordinary"[21] presides, which transcends urban ideals and comes close to being familiar. But this exploration is not possible without looking into the more challenging conditions of Tokyo, such as the lack of "sensory, environmental or democratic qualities."[22] The means with which we can understand informality and appropriation processes also play out in front of a larger global phenomenon. Alienation and what we call "the conditions of being in the world" define our needs, desires, and social interactions, which transcend the way we occupy space. Chapter Two then explores more detailed notions of materiality and matter. In this discussion, the principle of Oku is particularly interesting for unpacking the understated ecologies of Tokyo's fragmented urban spaces.

These performative qualities will be contextualized in Part Two, where we discuss voids as spatial capital in the larger urban environment. Chapter Three identifies conditions and processes that contribute to the production of vacant space in this vast megalopolis. We identify recent trends such as Japan's rapid demographic change, but also socioeconomic conditions and policy frameworks that are grounded on much earlier developments. On a smaller scale, there are road-widening projects to make traffic more effective and the neighborhood safer in the event of fires and earthquakes, as well as subdivision and fragmentation of plots. Further, land reclamation occurs to accommodate waste, and becomes new land that might become stalled in its development, creating an example of simultaneous growth and decline.

These processes of transformation, fragmentation, growth, and decline all occur simultaneously in Tokyo. While Japan might be in a state of economic decline, there are nonetheless mega investments, for example in building sites for the 2020 Olympics. The cited near-ness and now-ness is real across all levels and types of spaces.

This aspect sets Tokyo apart from conditions of decline in Detroit or Leipzig, and conditions of stalled growth in the Middle East. We will illustrate the implications of these processes as dynamic constructs in Chapter Three.

How is it possible to see something that is not part of modern developments or contemporary discussion, something that is part of a cycle, a "natural component of every dynamically evolving city,"[23] a reaction to a particular development strategy, something that is not permanent, something that is not wanted—but still offers the capacity to contribute to urban design strategies, to expose urban ecosystems, to operate as catalysts for creative practices—if it is understood in its own reality? As Waley states in "Re-scripting the City": "Tokyo had changed, as all cities do, but with greater rapidity. Equally, and more significantly, the ways in which the city is represented have changed."[24] The aspect of time and simultaneity allows us to treat Tokyo as a laboratory in which a closer investigation of multiple processes and their effects occurs. For us, void is an ephemeral object, a site—yet not only a space—but also a possible future and a counter-perspective on a predictable city. Tokyo's voids are possibilities in absence, flexible in time and space through their reading and performance.

PART ONE

The Performance of Tokyo's Vacant Space

Derelict sites, abandoned places, and vacancy assert a level of discomfort that is both appealing and repulsive at the same time. In his 2009 article "Anxious Landscapes: From the Ruin to Rust," Picon asks:

> How is it that, turning our back on several centuries of tradition that generally associated the contemplation of landscape with the idea of certain peace of mind, we are so often disconcerted, indeed even anxiety-ridden, by landscapes of this type?[1]

He outlines our emotional states of reading derelict sites by pointing to the disconnection between our images and interpretation of the landscape and the reality. Essentially, our fears, anxiety, and excitement regarding voids are rooted in the perceived nonperformance that defines these spaces. They don't function—at least momentarily—in the system that we have assigned to them through our codes and norms. They simply do not make sense. Referring to a study conducted by researchers at Penn Medical School about the relation of health and vacant land, Hamblin writes that our unease with vacancy stems from the "sense of loss of control that vacant properties impart."[2] Therefore, we try to assign alternative meanings and readings to those sites by highlighting the entities that emphasize and celebrate their otherness.

Accepting the condition that these spaces operate outside of our normative productive systems allows us to find new approaches to dealing with these sites, thus stimulating their activation. For instance, in places were vacancy has such a severe impact on the health and safety of neighborhoods, residents start to actively engage in "measures to adopt properties, clear them of dangerous stuff, turn them into hanging gardens, etc.,"[3] rather than just rely on authorities. Consequently, urban voids start to perform in different ways. In Part One, we explore the performances of Tokyo's urban voids through two lenses. The first chapter looks at ways in which these sites are approached, both formally and informally, as means of programmed space for inhabitation, appropriation, play, and experience. The second chapter explores spaces that perform as material-space and matter through ground, atmospheres, and vegetation.

In principle, urban voids can be framed as sites. The notion of site forms the expectation that something will occur to change the space. This might occur formally in design and development processes, or informally through appropriation and informal uses. These types of uses and processes assume a human intervention on or with the space. The spatial makeup of urban voids—often defined by remnants, ruins, or simply the nondesigned nature—forms a stark contrast to programmed urban spaces defined by typological labels such as "park" or "car park."

This contrast to a programmed and predictable urban environment seems to make urban voids attractive as alternative spaces offering spatial and social freedom in the otherwise homogeneous urban landscape, as reflected by the current discourse in urban design and landscape architecture.

Formalized development of vacant sites in the form of architectural, landscape architectural, or urban design interventions stands in stark contrast to informal, user-led appropriation. Luc Lévesque argues that, assuming positioned design responses take the site and its precondition as terrain vague into consideration, formalized approaches are challenged by those forces that initially produced these spaces.[4] The challenge lies in the fundamentally different nature of destructive forces on the one hand, and growth characterized as the intention for new development, on the other hand. This may mean exposing failure, or negating a site by eradication and a blank canvas approach.

While Solà-Morales and Lévesque argue for the need for a dualistic architectural response to terrain vague that takes site into consideration, we point to another challenge that formal design has to address. Reminiscences of the past, which transport the underlying memories of the derelict site—both tangible and intangible—will not necessarily be what we commonly describe as beautiful or useful. Although various design theorists have pointed to a necessary shift in perspective when thinking about aesthetic values and expressions of disrupted landscapes,[5] there are only a few examples that demonstrate an innovative approach to designing new landscapes beyond the glorified artifacts. The design professions still have to find their way in meaningfully approaching these challenges.

What if we consider urban voids as performative themselves—through own conditions of ground, atmospheres, microclimate, vegetation, and matter that make up the space?

The consideration of theses landscape attributes blurs the definition of void as nonperforming space even further. The spaces may be void of programmatic function, yet they are still performing in an ecologic capacity and as part of larger urban landscape systems. There is a type of nature, permeating through the cracks in the urban surface. If we foreground these cracks and the weeds colonizing them, we can start to trace a very different map of Tokyo; a map that shows the connections of ground makeup and vegetation relative to context. Most importantly, this map will be a representation of noninterference, and will show the conditions that emerge through processes embedded in the context of voids—without design, maintenance, or program.

One further aspect embedded in this view is very seductive: the atmospheric, grittiness, and dark aesthetic of voids that evoke our curiosity. What lies behind this fascination? Is it the contrast of wildness that these places suggest in the urban context that draws us in? How do we deal with this in Tokyo, where the nature of nothingness that extrudes from these spaces almost forms a sacred encounter? These perceptions transcend the performative ideas of use and matter to a metaphysical level as transmitters of the ephemeral: moments that we see in a ray of light on a cracked surface will engrain within us a deep personal memory and image of Tokyo.

CHAPTER 1

Intervention, Transgression, and Appropriation

One aspect of the current discourse on interstitial spaces is concerned with the temporary use of abandoned places. Urban vacant spaces have somehow become synonymous with the idea of informal appropriation as a widely applied tactic in reclaiming unused land, and, increasingly, as a new approach for community-driven urban redevelopment. The reclamations of vacant land as territories range from subversive actions that are conventionally pushed to hidden places in the city, to widely accepted and appreciated interventions of the so-called creative class, who enjoy the regulatory freedom of these spaces.

While this trend has long been established in the European and North American contexts, Tokyo is not widely known for temporary activations such as gardens, galleries, bars, and ski schools, and so far only very urban voids have been activated. Out of the roughly 180 urban voids documented in the Tokyo Void project,[1] only a handful support innovative temporary uses. One reason for this, we suggest, is that in contrast to other places, Tokyo's urban voids are typically very small. As discussed in the introduction, Japanese cities are inherently defined by smallness and inwardness.

Large-scale concepts are somewhat alien to that environment and therefore do not seem entirely applicable to the cultural and spatial context. As a consequence, vacant sites remain largely hidden and unnoticed.

While contemporary vacant spaces are not on the radar of the wider public audience, the Japanese people still have fond memories of *Harappa* (open field, wild field). Harappa is frequently cited in association with void spaces and seems to function as a code for instantly grasping the capacity the spaces offer: playgrounds for exploration and games. The term reflects a cultural nostalgia: an innocent childhood memory of the abundance of overgrown, open, and vacant spaces dispersed through cities after World War II, which children would conquer for play and adventure. The much-loved manga and anime character Doraemon—whose name is derived from *dora neko* (stray cat)—exemplifies the practice of uninhibited child's play and the excitement of otherness. Although he is in fact a robotic cat from the future that can produce all sorts of futuristic gadgets, he likes to roam harappa spaces with his human friends. Here, harappa spaces serve as meeting spots and baseball fields.

Children playing on vacant land
Taito-ku, North-West Tokyo, 2010

Since then, the ground for outdoor play has disappeared. Doraemon, who was created in 1969, has vanished from harappa sites, and the shift to more organized, indoor play activities has left the capacity of harappa unused. Most harappa have been reconstructed and, as in many other cities around the world, many sites that remain vacant are transformed into temporary parking spaces. This reality, however, does not deny new and emerging practices of creative temporary uses and informal appropriation that manifest in surprising ways.

Urban Void, Akabanenishi, Kita-Ku, Tokyo 2010
The large open space of a former public housing estate remains inacessible.

Today, there is an increasing number of alternative practices and temporary activation of vacant spaces in Tokyo. Citizens often go through lengthy processes of carefully negotiating their project plans with property owners, rather than appropriating spaces with spontaneous guerilla tactics. Although the overall amount may still be comparatively low in a global context, these pop-up spaces point to a significant change in the Japanese society in two ways. First, there is the rise of a more active and creative society as an increasing number of people develop an improved environmental awareness and an appreciation for traditional social and cultural values, which have been lost or forgotten in the decades when the country focused on economic growth. Second, the success of the pop-up spaces points to a shift in attitudes towards outdoor recreation and public open space in general.

Formal design approaches also start to show how the economic and environmental decline and associated problems over the past decades have led to the repurposing of sites that were intended to perform quite differently. In addition, amazing and unique everyday practices of utilizing urban voids appear, which are tightly linked to the tradition of informal appropriation and shape large parts of Tokyo. These practices provide a deep insight into cultural codes of territory and community roles that are imperative to working with flexible conditions and uncertain ownership structures that define Tokyo's voids.

All projects, and the significant changes they bring, are only apparent in contrast to conventional practices and preconceptions of urban open and public space in Tokyo.

What role does open space play in Tokyo? In this aspect, the neighborhood park forms a springboard to discover the landscape of everyday Tokyo. The insight into the context of Tokyo's landscape, the spatial use, and appropriation suggests that we may need to question what we perceived as scarcity. The uses and functions, which the pop-up spaces in particular fulfill, point to shifting desires towards active and consumer-oriented spaces. The event city extends to urban voids. Through this new understanding, ideas of formal performative aspects and normative interpretation of public space through typology, labels such as "park" may need to be reconsidered.

New Approaches

In a highly regulated environment such as Tokyo, vacant spaces offer an opportunity to explore activities that require specific spatial setups and conditions, or are otherwise restricted or prohibited in official public spaces. While very few projects take a provocative stand, many indirectly critique the use of Tokyo's urban space and the loss of environmental qualities and social values. Thus, it is not surprising to see so many projects that aim for citizen participation, increasing communication, and community spirit, and that provide a platform for experimentation. Another common theme runnning through most projects is the idea of revisiting traditional trades and craftsmanship as inherent parts of the Japanese culture. Activities on vacant spaces often include workshops or short events that offer people the opportunity to explore and rediscover special techniques and skills in relation to construction, crafting, or food production.

One extraordinary example is the Ginza Rice Farm, a project that represents a revived interest in cultural values in form of traditional farming practices. Initiated in 2009 by Kazumi Iimura, a trained architect turned farmer, the project aimed to raise awareness for the rice farming techniques by transforming a one-hundred-square-meter vacant space into a temporary rice paddy. For a little longer than half a year, Tokyoites could engage in planting, maintaining, and harvesting rice, and could learn more about sustainable food production. Special techniques included the introduction of a duck family for weeding and fertilizing the paddy. In addition, this temporary green space attracted lots of insects, and subsequently frogs and birds. The large photo tapestry surrounding the plot included further information on the diversity of rice species, their cultivation requirements, and growing areas in Japan.

As if a rice field in the middle of Tokyo were not be surprising enough, what really made this project outstanding was its location in a backstreet of Tokyo's fashionable Ginza district. This neighborhood still has the most expensive land prices in Japan, and has an equal standing to Fifth Avenue in New York.

New Approaches:
Farmers Market, 246 Common, Aoyama, Minato-ku

Ginza Rice Farm

1 Chome-6-7 Ginza
Chūō-ku, Tōkyō-to

Type:	*vacant building plot*
Ownership:	*private*
Use:	*rice farm and education venue*
Size:	*86 m²*
Duration:	*May–October 2010*
Current status:	*six-story golf retail shop*

In 2009, architect-farmer Kazumi Iimura initiated the Ginza Rice farm project with the aim to bring an understanding of the deep-rooted culture of rice farming back to the city. A small vacant plot in a backstreet in Ginza, Tokyo's most expensive retail district, became available for this project after sucessful negotiations with landowners and tax attorneys.
For a six-month period the plot became farm, class room and festival stage. Ducks were introduced to maintain weeds in the water filled rice terrace: the rice was grown, harvested, cooked, and sold as Onigiri rice balls on site. Planting and harvesting festivals attracted people to the site, which also became a spot for lunchtime breaks.

0
100
200
300
400
500 m

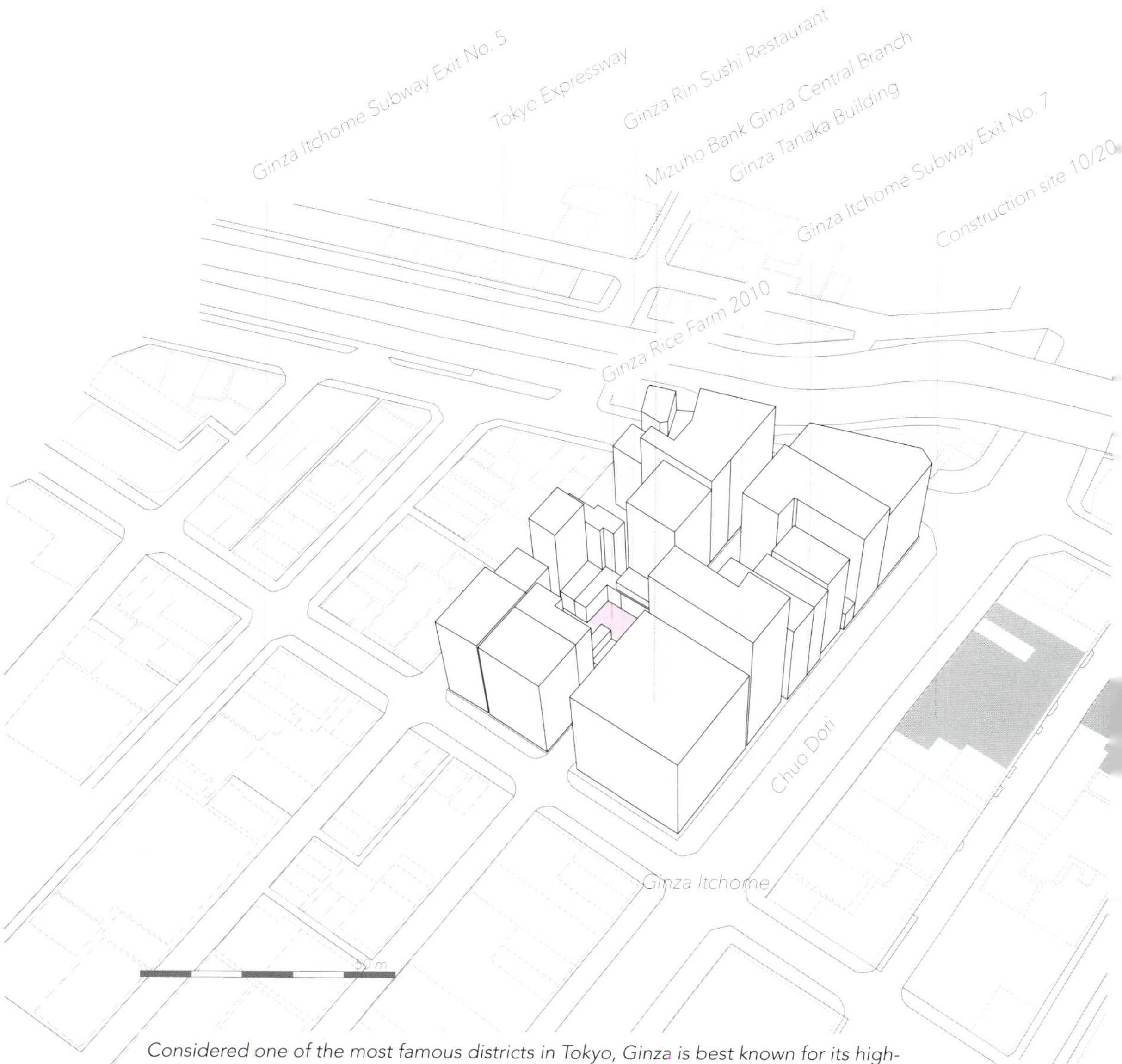

Considered one of the most famous districts in Tokyo, Ginza is best known for its high-end retail business that line both sides of the main street-Chuo Dori. Attractive to both domestic and international tourists, the boulevard is closed to the traffic on Sundays, providing a unique experience to enjoy the district while strolling between the big retail palaces. This traditional shopping and entertainment district has undergone constant redevelopments since its early days. The most recent renovations of leading international luxury brands by star architects have also put this location on the radar of architects and design community. The urban grid pattern of the district is largely determined by three aspects: front sides that are dominated by large-scale glitter and pomp; backstreets lined

Ginza Rice Farm, 2010
View out to illuminated backstreet shops from the harvested rice field on a chilly October night

with smaller exclusive crafts shops and restaurants; and permeating alleys that lie behind both as the hidden side of the district in the form of dark and often dirty passages that lead to secret bars and hidden shrines. In a district with one of the highest land prices in Tokyo, the diversity is surprising. This structure of extreme contrasts is also reflected in the existing void spaces. Spaces facing the main boulevard are often immediately redeveloped into high-end real estate. In the smaller backstreets and alleyways, however, gaps start to appear. While in some cases these sites are transformed into lucrative coin-parking, it is not uncommon to see undeveloped building plots remaining vacant for several years.

The location was the result of a six-month negotiation process in which Kazuki Iimura lobbied with tax attorneys and accountants to find a metropolitan vacant space for the rice farm. Although the details of the deal between Iimura and the landlord are not confirmed, we suggest that the Japanese taxation system supported the temporary use of the site.[2] In Japan, unused land is taxed at higher rates than land used for building or agricultural production, providing incentive for transforming vacant spaces even temporarily.[3] Hence, it may only be a question of time until more projects like the Ginza Rice Farm emerge in Tokyo.

While the success and attraction of the Ginza Rice Farm lies in introducing a low-key rice paddy into Tokyo's most fashionable shopping district, and explicitly contrasting the materiality and usage of space to its surrounding context, Kasu Harappa Ondi reflects a project that strongly connects with the particular structure and demographic of its neighborhood. By focusing on aspects of livability, this project tries to return something to the local community, in order to explicitly contribute to the overall neighborhood quality.

Kasu Harappa Ondi translates as rental vacant space. This site is located in the quiet neighborhood of Yanaka—a beautiful neighborhood of low-rise residential housing, shops, and temples. With fifty-three square meters, this site represents one of the vacant spaces that are so ubiquitous in Tokyo, and blends so well into the surrounding context that one could pass it without even recognizing its rather unusual setup. Only a thin rope indicates the demarcation line between public and private, and with its graveled surface, cleared of any major vegetation, we could easily misread the site as ordinary vacant space waiting for development, or as a parking lot for the residents living nearby.

However, the owners deliberately set aside the financially lucrative coin-operated parking option, and instead placed a higher value on the spatial quality of the neighborhood. Appreciating Yanaka's history of cultural and creative richness, they decided to contribute to the neighborhood atmosphere. In recent years, Yanaka has become a new focus for the creative scene exemplified by the increasing number of galleries, workshops, and cafes selling handicraft and artworks. Ondi contributes to this environment by providing an outdoor gallery space that local artists, performers, and other creative people can rent at a minimal fee for events and exhibitions.

Although the concept of a gallery space perfectly fits into Yanaka's creative atmosphere, Ondi is anything but an ordinary gallery. Only simple rules outline the terms of use, enabling prospective users to take full responsibility for their events, while also providing maximum freedom as to how the space can be used. This offers the possibility for a diverse mix of events—ranging from performances, demonstrations, art exhibitions, and cultural celebrations, to market events and student workshops. The idea behind Ondi is to provide a space that supports conversation and invites everyone to participate. During the events, the site transforms into an open stage, without walls and roof, while the street turns into a theater where strolling residents and visitors become part of the audience. Here, everybody has the opportunity to participate in the event instead of just remaining a spectator of the artwork.

With its exposure to the elements, Ondi also opens discussions about the physical qualities and materiality of Tokyo's vacant spaces. The project name plays with the association surrounding the words harappa and *Ondi* (音地). The latter translates as "sound of soil" and refers to the appreciation of its natural beauty. A Butoh dance performance, held on site in the summer of 2009, exemplified this quality of depth and openness in the unsealed surface. During the performance, the strangeness of light and shadow reflected in wet dirt met with the often absurd and extreme expressions of Butoh and created an experiential quality of the play that could hardly have been achieved on a conventional theater stage. It is precisely these material qualities that offer real momentum for unpredictable, serendipitous activity and experiences in Tokyo—a city dominated by concrete and asphalt.

Since Ondi's inception in 2006, the number of activities on the site has increased significantly. Today, Ondi hosts events almost every weekend during the year. The increasing interest among ordinary Tokyoites who host and participate in these events not only demonstrates the popularity of this project, but also reflects the immense potential of alternative practices as inspiration for creative action and bringing people together. With its low profile, Ondi realizes its vision of a lively and engaging neighborhood and provides a viable activation strategy appropriate to Tokyo's urban and cultural condition.

Kasu Harappa ONDI

Yanaka, Taito-ku, Tokyo, Japan 110–0001

Type:	*vacant building plot*
Ownership:	*private*
Use:	*public gallery, market, and event space*
Size:	*53 m^2*
Duration:	*ongoing since 09/2006*

The "rental vacant space" Ondi was conceived by architects Toshiyuki Makizumi and Yoshiko Yanai in 2006. Originally planned as a site for a residential project, Ondi evolved into a space that reflects the creative context of the neighbourhood.
For a small fee, the small site can be rented for activities—such as markets, performances, exhibitions, installations, and crafts workshops—and has been continuously booked since 2009.
Ondi is a key initiative in Yanaka, it supports local NPO activities such as Yanaka Gakko (the school of Yanaka) and invites conversations between artists, performers, schoolkids, and residents through the various types of activities on site.

0
100
200
300
400
500 m

Yanaka is a small-scale Tokyo neighborhood, located in Taito ward, a historic district six kilometers north of the center. Marked by an abundance of temples, shrines, and cemeteries, this area provides a unique landscape with a significant amount of green space, including large trees that are otherwise unseen in most parts of the city. With its large number of mature cherry trees, the Yanaka cemetery is one of Tokyo's most popular places for recreation—not only during the hanami (cherry blossom viewing) season in spring. Otherwise, the area is dominated by low-rise residential properties and small retail and manufacturing businesses.

Kasu Harappa Ondi on a Sunday afternoon

Adjacent to three major universities and art schools, Yanaka has always been a popular place for academics and artists, enriching the neighborhood with a diverse creative scene. In recent years, this seems to have expanded with more art galleries and small cafes emerging. Although gentrification processes can be observed, Yanaka has so far been able to retain its fine-grained urban fabric and distinct cultural character, especially along major roads.

Kasu Harappa Ondi: Yanaka Peke and photo market

Kasu Harappa Ondi: Yanaka Peke and photo market

Kasu Harappa Ondi: Yurt construction workshop

Kasu Harappa Ondi: Yanaka PEKE and Sunday market

Kasu Harappa Ondi: Sunday market

Kasu Harappa Ondi: University workshop and exhibition

Kasu Harappa Ondi: Yurt construction workshop

Kasu Harappa Ondi: Yurt construction workshop

Kasu Harappa Ondi: Butoh performance

Kasu Harappa Ondi: Craft workshop

Kasu Ha-appa Ondi: University workshop and exhibition

Kasu Harappa Ondi: University workshop and exhibition

Formalized Design Strategies

As many authors claim, it seems particularly difficult for the discipline of architecture to find a meaningful approach to void spaces without falling back into common practice and focus on form generation, aesthetics, and productivity.[4] Although other disciplines—such as landscape architecture or urban design—may not focus on form generation and aesthetics as much as architecture, they still rely inherently on economic forces and commercial outputs. This reliance raises the question of whether a design response to terrain vague is in fact at all possible, or whether economic and commercial imperatives inevitably mean that a design response finds itself in opportunistic domains.

While the concept of embracing roughness, incompletion, and subversive natural qualities in designs is relatively new to architecture,[5] there are some promising landscape architectural examples of the transformation of derelict, abandoned spaces. Richard Haag's Gas Work Park in Seattle—dating from the nineteen-seventies—could be regarded as one of the first projects to actively engage discussion about the qualities of derelict industrial sites and design interventions. More recent examples increasingly expand these design explorations: Latz & Partner, Landscape Park Duisburg-Nord, 1994; Gilles Clement, Derborence Island in the Park Henri Mattise, Lille, 1995; James Corner Field Operations, Fresh Kills, from 2007 and the New York High Line, 2009; Fugmann & Janotta, Park am Nordbahnhof, Berlin, 2009; or D.I.R.T Studio, Urban Outfitters Headquarters, Philadelphia, 2005–2011. In embracing the distinct character of roughness, ugliness, and otherness, these formally designed projects challenge conventional notions of the aesthetics and functionality of parks, industrial sites, and vacant land in metropolitan cities. The particular quality in these projects lies in the sensitive balance between space and time. The design only sets the spatial framework in which natural processes occur, while the site is in constant transformation, unpredictable and unfinished, providing the possibility for a different kind of environmental and spatial experience.

The common characteristics of these projects are the orientation towards large-scale territories: the reclamation of abandoned, often polluted, postindustrial sites, transformed into recreational public spaces. In consequence, these projects become substantial drivers for tourism for both local and international travelers. Here, the interstitial reflects more than a mere site—a small, hidden unit in the urban fabric. Although still part of a larger urban context, these places transcend into independent landscapes that inhabit their very own spatial, functional, ecological systems.

One large-scale reclamation project in Tokyo that falls into this category is Umi no Mori (The Sea Forest), initiated by the famous Japanese architect Tadao Ando in collaboration with the Tokyo Metropolitan Government.

Umi no Mori is part of the so-called Inner Central Break Water Reclamation Area, a group of landfill sites in Tokyo Bay. The site is one of the newer islands—created between 1973 and 1987 out of almost 12.3 million tons of garbage covered with surplus soil from the city's construction sites—and rises thirty meters above sea level. In contrast to older developments in Tokyo Bay, Umi no Mori is intended to represent the next generation of land reclamation. Originally launched as part of Tokyo's bid for the 2016 Summer Olympics, the idea behind this project is to transform this artificial island into a gigantic urban forest.

Empowered by the image of sustainability and citizen participation, Ando envisions this project to become a worldwide symbol for recycling; a symbiosis between the forest and people, the city and nature. Very much in the Japanese tradition of ***Muda, Mura, Muri*** (Waste Not, Want Not), it is intended that all materials and processes used on site will be recycled and recyclable resources. The foundation for the forest is composed of soils and sludge generated from water purification and sewage treatment, which are mixed with compost from organic materials obtained from the maintenance of park and street trees. In addition, methane gases produced during garbage disintegration will be collected and used as fuel for power generation.[6]

Almost as redemption for other investment-driven developments in the area, Umi no Mori turns to citizens to actively engage in this project. Under the campaign slogan "not for us, but for our children,"[7] the Tokyo Metropolitan Government asks for private donations to provide the financial resources for the 480,000 plant seedlings necessary to create the large eighty-eight-hectare forest. Local elementary schools participate hands-on in the plant propagation and planting. Children and other volunteers also have the opportunity to participate in the occasional planting event, often alongside celebrities like Bono or Ando himself. Supported by massive media attention, citizen engagement has been quite successful. Only eighteen months after the city government officially launched the project in 2007, individual donations had reached already almost two-thirds of the expected figure.

In 2009, Tokyo lost its bid to host the Olympic Games in 2016 and media coverage of the project significantly dropped. Then it was a question of whether the future and success of Umi no Mori were really as independent from the Games as Ando claimed.[8] Yet in a renewed bid Tokyo won and will host the Games in 2020 and the Sea Forest will play an important role as venue for equestrian and mountain biking events. The facilities for canoeing and kayaking competitions will even remain a permanent facility as part of the Olympic Legacy.

Minato-ku, Shiodome

Umi no Mori: The Sea Forest

What is evident, however, is that Ando's ambition for the project is much bigger than the final outcome. Umi no mori is only one of a few planting projects initiated by the architect, which encourages community participation. Ando understands these projects as a response to dramatic societal changes and social disintegration brought to Japanese cities by modernism. According to Ando, modern architecture imposed homogeneous and meaningless designs that failed to support communication, human interaction, and healthy neighborhoods. "I believe that these disasters have been deeply linked [to] the fact that we are losing beautiful scenery in our society,"[9] the scenery created from memories and embodied experiences of calming and comforting nature. In pursuing this sentiment, Ando's projects seek to recover lost spatial, social, and environmental structures, while providing citizens with a new sense of empowerment.

Consciously embracing the dimension of time, Umi no Mori exerts another novelty in Tokyo's urban development. The basic planting framework of the forest is planned to be in place by 2017—ten years after the project's launch. Full completion is expected around 2037. Rather than focusing on the final product, the project communicates through processes, transformation, and growth. Paradoxically, this also demonstrates Umi no Mori's limitations, because it remains unclear what the project will offer to the community after its completion. Current available renderings present an immaculate image of an island fully covered in a homogeneous green blanket—an aesthetic idealization of a forest that seems frozen in time. These perfect images do not communicate a vision for activity within the forest and how residents may use it. Neither do they convey a sense of time and processes—such as growth, maturing, decay—or the impact of harvesting and maintenance.

We have come to some understanding of the immense potential of void spaces, citizen participation, and time in a city like Tokyo, particularly at this massive scale. In Umi no Mori, there is a vast vacant space with immense potential, on the one hand. On the other hand, all events in the project conform to a strict choreography that allows no opportunity for spontaneous actions and unpredictable outcomes. The project is clearly quite unique and inspirational in is setup, design, and dedication to the community and environment. Nevertheless, there is a real danger that after its completion, the forest will not offer much more than other public parks in Tokyo. Its contribution to the urban landscape may remain symbolic due to its isolation and distance from the city. The aspiration for a symbiosis between the forest, people, city, and nature—so desperately needed in the Tokyo—might not progress beyond the creation of "beautiful scenery" in Tokyo Bay, far away from the conditions of the everyday.

Urban Void, Chuo-ku, Tokyo 2012
The large open space, surrounded by fences, remains an inacessible wilderness.

Tokyo's Everyday Landscape

The full potential of the previous projects can only be understood in the context of Tokyo's public space and the everyday landscape of the city. A Google image search for "Tokyo Park" brings up stunning images of Tokyo's three main green spaces: Ueno Park, Shinjuku-Gyoen, and the beautiful forest of the Meiji Shrine. These places operate in the same fashion as Umi no Mori—event spaces that are highly frequented over the weekend. However, the reality of neighborhood parks, much closer to the everyday life of residents is rather bleak, as upsettingly exemplified in the 2008 film, *Tokyo Sonata*.[10]

The film focuses on the social paralysis and alienation that permeate Japanese contemporary society. At the beginning, the protagonist—a family man with two sons—loses his job and finds himself in a nondescript urban park in Tokyo, where he meets countless other suit-wearing, laid-off salarymen. Each one sits in silence staring into the air, drinking canned coffee, smoking, waiting for the 5 PM bell to ring so that they can go home, pretending to return from work. He goes back to the park every day, keeping up a routine of pretense because of his shame in admitting the loss of his job.

Miyashita Park, Shibuya
Atelier Bow-Wow, 2011

Miyashita Park is a controversial transformation project funded in part by Nike. Protest groups opposed the converting of Miyashita Park into a consumer-oriented "NIKE Park." It was estimated that 150 homeless people lived at the site prior its modernization. The site now is locked over night and includes footsal courts and climbing walls. The concrete play animals are reminiscent of Tokyo's neighborhood parks.

The park in this scene is essentially not much more than a paved surface next to an elevated expressway, furnished only with a few bollards, each with space enough for one person to sit. It resembles the prototype of Tokyo's contemporary urban park.

Numerous scholars have written about the differences in conceptualizing public space in Japan and pointed to distinct types of spaces that historically take the function of public space (i.e., streets, alleyways, and bathhouses).

The authors argue that different cultural framings have led to the understanding that public spaces in the form of parks are conceived as amenities provided by the government, rather than spaces for liberation from the state.[11] Other factors, such as the infamous Japanese work routines and commuting times, have been associated with the poor usage of parks. In other words, public urban space is a foreign concept in Japan and the conclusion is that Japanese people, thus, do not have an inherent desire to use public spaces or do not understand how to use them. However, looking at the quintessential park that appears in *Tokyo Sonata,* we can argue that the poor design quality and the countless restrictions, which define contemporary parks today, are the main deterrent when it comes to their usability.

Tokyo's 1956 Urban Parks Act stipulates a methodical distribution of urban parks to achieve a minimum supply of open space for Tokyo's inhabitants. According to this scheme, parks in Tokyo mainly function as evacuation space to mitigate the effects of earthquake disasters. Standard distances between parks are devised so that for every one square kilometer, at least one medium-sized park and four small parks should be provided. Assuming a population of 40,000 people, one additional large park is introduced every four square kilometers. The minimal size for a small park is not defined in this framework, but it is not unusual to classify parks as small as thirty square meters. The official classification system is also interesting: not only are there city or ward parks, but also child amusement parks, temporary child parks, and pocket parks or plazas.

Many of Tokyo's neighborhood parks were established between 1970 and 1990, predominantly as play spaces. Even in older parks, originally designed as multifunctional spaces, the government later added play equipment to provide play spaces for the baby boomer generation. Today, the quality and appearance of small parks has significantly deteriorated due to poor maintenance. With a shrinking birth rate and an aging society, the demand for play spaces has decreased dramatically compared to a few decades ago, but the swings, slides, and spring rockers have never been rebuilt to facilitate other programs and uses for a different demographic populations. Considering the small and medium-sized neighborhood parks, it is almost possible to describe another void: the true nonspace. While these parks are designed to provide public and green space functions, their capacity in these terms is often extremely low. A 2008 study of the design quality of all 146 neighborhood parks in four wards of Tokyo (Taito, Toshima, Meguro, and Bunkyo) found that only twenty-four of these parks could be described as possessing positive tendencies in their design quality. Positive tendencies were defined by spatial quality in composition of internal elements, quality of vegetation, and the quality of the surrounding context. The remaining 122 parks were found to be either the standard park layout as stipulated by the 1956 Urban Park act, as seen in *Tokyo Sonata,* or spaces that were normally not classifiable as parks: street-side hedges including a bench; a fenced-in, rusting see-saw on a street; or barren land under the expressway only identifiable as park by its prohibited-uses sign.[12]

Homeless people account for the main user group of Tokyo's public parks.[13] According to a report on homelessness published in 2013 by the Japanese Ministry of Health, Labor and Welfare—in collaboration with the Ministry of Land, Transport and Infrastructure—29.7 percent of homeless people indicated that they were living in public parks.[14] Another 29.1 percent indicated they were sleeping on riverbanks. Apart from policies and actions to decrease the overall number of homeless people, local city governments have also started retrofitting parks to discourage their use as shelters and sleeping places. Measures include fencing off areas that would allow informal settling; limiting seating to one-person seats; and restricting access and stay. In exposed public places, only subtle traces reveal inhabitation through the presence of neatly stacked piles of cardboard hidden behind bushes. On riverbanks and in areas under bridges and expressways, the inhabitation is clearly visibly, however, through countless cardboard boxes covered in blue tarp. Against the popular belief that vacant spaces would attract less appreciated members of the public, including homeless people, vacant lots do not seem to function as spaces for temporal inhabitation. Given that some voids are easily accessible and only fenced off by a piece of string, and others offer secluded spaces behind metal walls, this noninterference seems surprising at first glance. But the Japanese culture of politeness and deep respect forbids intruding into other people's property.

This awareness extends through all classes and social statuses and contributes to the fact that Tokyo is one of the safest metropolises in the world. Informal practices and appropriation are deeply ingrained in daily activities that profoundly shape the urban realm. But these practices occur in Tokyo at much subtler level than in many other places around the world. "Informal extensions" of private spaces into the public sphere are rooted in distinct historical aspects, such as the legacy of shared spaces and utilities in semiprivate public spaces of *roji* (traditional alleyways). One prominent manifestation of this informal extension is Tokyo's flowerpot gardens. Residents in dense low-rise neighborhoods traditionally practice informal gardening with mobile flowerpot arrangements, and these extraordinary hybrid landscapes of individual gardening creativity define entire streetscapes.

In contrast to guerilla gardening, this practice is not based on a political motivation, but on the desire to beautify ones own home and to engage with the pastime activity of gardening. The effect that a garden, made from potted plants, has on the neighboring community is desirable but it is not the main ambition for most of the gardeners. Nevertheless, this tradition of shared, informally reclaimed space produces green, livable, and socially rich community spaces.[15] Often, the informal flowerpot gardens are the only greenery found in areas that otherwise lack open green space.

Small Neighborhood Parks

Tokyo's public parks largely consist of small neighborhood parks. The design and distribution of the small parks are strongly influenced by policy requirements to provide open space as evacuation sites and to mitigate disaster in earthquake-prone Tokyo. The ubiquitous play equipment remains a feature of the long-gone baby-boom era. The desire to provide multifunctional spaces that cater to young children and provide disaster relief produces uniform and often desolate spaces.

台東区
千
せん

Tokyo's Informal Gardens
Entire streetscapes are shaped by informal gardening practices.

Where the informal gardens encroach on the public realm, for example on roads and footpaths, this use of shared space is carefully negotiated between neighbors—in general, nonverbally—through subtle adaptations, rather than removing or destroying the potted plants. The respect for the property and the respect for the investment in community—for instance, by beautifying areas of neglect through potted plants—prevent interference with the informally extended territories through vandalism. In addition, the informal street-side gardens exemplify socially established rules and norms for sharing spatial resources as a common good.

Given the abundance of street-side flowerpot gardens, a pragmatic assumption is that urban voids frequently function as gardens. Although the occasional flowerpot may encroach on neighboring vacant land, only a few voids are really used as gardens. In one instance of mapping urban voids in Kita-ku, we came across an elderly lady tending three potted plants placed on a vacant site adjacent to her home. She was very apologetic and explained that she placed her plants only temporarily outside and that she had no intention of disturbing the vacant plot.

Even so, dynamic processes of informal uses sometimes extend to the appropriation of vacant spaces in ordered and negotiated form. Domestic uses that traditionally occurred in shared spaces can also be observed in vacant spaces, and range from washing and drying clothes, to gardening, and storing and drying vegetables. Vacant lots and the fences surrounding the sites are frequently appropriated to provide services to the public, such as do-it-yourself garbage sorting systems, and do-it-yourself ashtrays made from cans that residents attach to the fences. In areas with commercial activity, shop owners reclaim fences as temporary display and storage space.

Concerns about safety and issues of cleanliness and their effect on the neighborhood character are global concerns that pervade every discussion about the value of vacant spaces. Tokyo is no exception in this regard. As one of the first countermeasures, people implement coin-operated parking facilities on vacant sites, which are financially very lucrative. Soerensen observes that "everywhere in the suburbs, parking lots are replacing fields and forest, as they are often the most lucrative temporary land use, and car ownership and use per capita continues to increase."[16] This issue is not limited to the suburbs, as the demand for parking space is even higher in inner-city neighborhoods and accounts for the main use of vacant spaces.

Until today, car ownership has not been overly attractive in Tokyo. In fact, Tokyo has the lowest car ownership rates in Japan with only thirty automobiles per one hundred inhabitants. In comparison, the figures for a car-dependent city like Melbourne, Australia show a whopping 91 percent of the residents own at least one car, and 16 percent of car owners possess even three or more cars. In Tokyo, effective public transport and walkable neighborhoods make car use unnecessary, and the notorious traffic congestion makes private drives more than unappealing. A further aspect resulting from Tokyo's extreme urban density is that purchasing a car requires proof of a car park. Occasionally, the car park is so far away from home that Tokyoites are placed the in the peculiar situations of having to catch a taxi to their parked car in order to take their car for a drive. A 2009 study by Tokyo University showed that most car owners in Tokyo would not use their car for commuting, but only for shopping and only to places that provide a parking spot.

Numerous companies specialize in coin-operated parking facilities and actively promote the temporary transformation of urban voids into "productive" commercial spaces. These firms offer a full-service package of paving and marking, deployment of signage, cashiers, and vending machines. The package options include calculation of the most profitable site layout and annual incomes generated by the car park, inclusion in GPS-based navigation maps for drivers that indicate real-time car parking availability, and servicing of the car park infrastructure. But the providers also take care of the initial preparation of the site, including the demolishing of derelict houses and clearing of the site—which, according to the operators, also clearly offer benefits beyond the obvious financial returns. Playing with the common perception that a derelict property attracts subversive activities that disrupt the orderly functioning of a neighborhood, the operators openly promote the construction of parking spaces for the sake of the community. If you replace the derelict building with coin-operated parking spaces, so the self-serving advertising goes, the misfits will have to move somewhere else. In this line of argument, coin-operated parking offers the only suitable safe and clean solution to maintain a neighborhood's integrity.

In 2005, the Tokyo-based designer architects mi-ri-meter offered a poignant critique to the increasing parking spaces. As a direct reference to the coin-operated businesses, they conceptualized and implemented a one-day coin-camping event on a vacant lot. The designers aimed to experiment with the lifestyle of "pay-as-you-go" for the urban population.[17] Similar to the events during the international annual Park(ing) Day, which takes over already established parking spaces, this project questions the commercialization and the vehicular consumption of urban space.

Lévesque characterizes the practice of temporary parking spaces as an urban expression that decries "the disorder (these spaces) represent in the city."[18] Tokyo's coin-operated parking spaces go even a step further, as they try to overcome the disorder on both macro and micro levels. On the macro level, the parking spaces neatly integrate into the urban material by avoiding the disruption of economic performance and productivity. On the micro level, they pretend a visual integrity through their immaculately designed surfaces and equipment. Often, this attempt is so overperformed that their immaculate bitumen appears a little too black, the markers a little too white. In this state of overperformance, the coin-operated parking spaces remain alien to their urban environment, inevitably appearing more void than terrain vague.

250¥/20 min.
parking spaces: 3
maxium profit: 54,000 ¥/day

500¥/20 min.
parking spaces: 5
maxium profit: 180,000 ¥/day

400¥/20 min.
parking spaces: 5
maxium profit: 144,000 ¥/day

500¥/30 min.
parking spaces: 15
maxium profit: 540,000 ¥/day

1500¥/1 hour
parking spaces: 3
maxium profit: 108,000 ¥/day

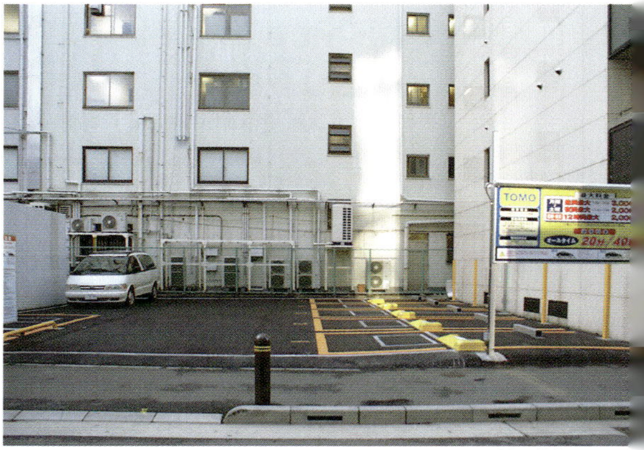

400¥/20 min.
parking spaces: 6
maxium profit: 172,800 ¥/day

700¥/30 min.
parking spaces: 2
maxium profit: 67,200 ¥/day

300¥/20 min.
parking spaces: 3
maxium profit: 43,200 ¥/day

500¥/15 min.
parking spaces: 5
maxium profit: 240,000 ¥/day

400¥/20 min.
parking spaces: 5
maxium profit: 144,000 ¥/day

500¥/30 min.
parking spaces: 5
maxium profit: 120,000 ¥/day

Coin parking in Ginza, 2011

Temporary vacant lots as coin parking spaces. This profitable use of vacancy is a key part of Ginza's traffic infrastructure where roadside parking is extremely limited. Most of the spaces documented here were redeveloped by 2014.

"Do We Still Need Parks?"[19]

In a 2002 essay published in *TOPOS* magazine, the Dutch landscape architect Hans Ophius provocatively asks whether in the contemporary urban context we would "still need parks." Ophius argues that classic park designs and programs may in fact be obsolete, since changes in people's lifestyles change the demand for outdoor recreation to different types of open spaces—namely, event spaces or less formal spaces allowing for nonprogrammed appropriation. His expansive question is applicable to Tokyo in a number of ways. What are the public's expectations, needs, and desires today regarding contemporary open spaces? Certainly, the image of a leisurely Sunday afternoon stroll in the park is no longer applicable—if in fact it ever was—in parks of less than 300 square meters.

Tokyo Picnic Club (TPC)[20] vividly engages the idea of active outdoor recreation in the metropolis. Through their picnic events, the group explores the conditions that enable picnics in Tokyo and offers a striking critique of contemporary parks in the city.

Tokyo Picnic Club (TPC) was founded by a group of architects and designers in 2002 to celebrate the bicentennial anniversary of picnic, established by the activities of "Pic-Nic Club" in London, March 1802. TPC defines picnic as a free and democratic activity, a joyful gathering where all are welcome as long as they bring gorgeous homemade food. The powerful message of TPC to "do your own picnic" invites critical engagement with urban and public space issues.

The picnic is a powerful metaphor for engaged use of outdoor space as social medium. It requires preparation, thought, creativity, the idea of a location, and social connectedness. TPC even goes so far as to critique Tokyo's ubiquitous convenience: instant food and unsustainable packaging. For their events, they do not allow plastic sheets to sit on, and all food has to be homemade. TPC is always searching for new places where they can hold their picnics. While they have never used a public park for their events, they have used larger vacant sites. What Tokyo Picnic Club and Ophuis' observations teach us is that the shift in the perception and use of public space sits within the user. The user brings desires for social interaction and leisure outdoors, and the space needs to function as a medium that allows multiple flexible uses. These ideas also refer back to the possibilities urban voids possess, the capacity to operate as nonprogrammed spaces that could fulfill alternative functions of public space.

The increasing number of pop-up spaces on vacant land demonstrates that Tokyoites have started to engage with these possibilities, often inspired by overseas examples of temporary activation. One such example is the 246 Common farmers' market, which took its inspiration from similar events in Portland, Oregon. The project is located in Aoyama—a stylish shopping and entertainment district popular with the younger generation—on a plot of land that was previously occupied by up-market restaurants and fashion retailers, such as Japanese designer Issey Miyake. Adjacent to the Aoyama Avenue, lined with large retail buildings, the 250-square-meter site is now awaiting reconstruction of a similar, big-footprint development.

A few blocks further to the north, there is an even larger area of vacant land. In the past few years, a small container bar opened its business in the northwest corner overlooking the rest of this massive void, which is temporarily occupied with the ubiquitous coin-operated parking spaces. The 246 Common could have easily turned into a similar development, but the organizers, who leased the spaces for three years, were more inclined to work towards the scale and community of the district. Dominated by small-scale, mix-use buildings with narrow, walkable backstreets winding down the Aoyama hills, this central area counts as one of the most beautiful neighborhoods in the city. The site is divided into two areas. The front part comprises food stalls that sell organically grown produce and trendy food and beverages of all types from containers and caravans. While this section demonstrates its international influence, the back site has a more unique Japanese expression. With its small, wooden pop-up stalls offering Japanese street food and handmade craft, wood chips that cover the ground, and planter beds that provide space for small trees and natural shade, this section resembles the intimate atmosphere of traditional merchant spaces.

It is this diversity and the intimate atmosphere that provide a place for encounter. Although 246 Common is a highly commercialized and lifestyle-oriented project, it may in fact offer more than the slightly superficial image it represents at first glance. The concept explicitly aims to promote interactions and communication by providing a recreation and meeting space for residents, workers, and visitors—similar to the traditional neighborhood organizations.[21] Whether this high aim can be achieved is questionable, but 246 Common certainly returns more to the community than other farmers' markets that only operate on weekends (e.g., the Aoyama Farmers Market in front of the United Nations University only a few blocks further south).

246 Common

Aoyama Minato-ku, Tokyo, Japan

Type:	*vacant building plot*
Ownership:	*private*
Use:	*commercial use, pop-up cafe, farmers' market, and workshop*
Size:	*appox. 800 m^2*
Duration:	*two-year lease 2012–2014*

246 Common forms a welcome resting spot for shoppers of nearby Omotesando street. Designed as a courtyard partly surrounded by container bars, small organic food stalls and central shared cafés provide champagne, mojitos, organic produce, and seating.
The space connects to a smaller laneway. There, temporary buildings, constructed utilizing building material salvaged from demolition sites, form an intimate setting.
246 Common is a commercial project that innovatively deals with vacancy through a critical agenda of bottom-up economies and sustainability.
In summer 2014, the space is vacant, the 246 Common, gone.

0 100 200 300 400 500 m

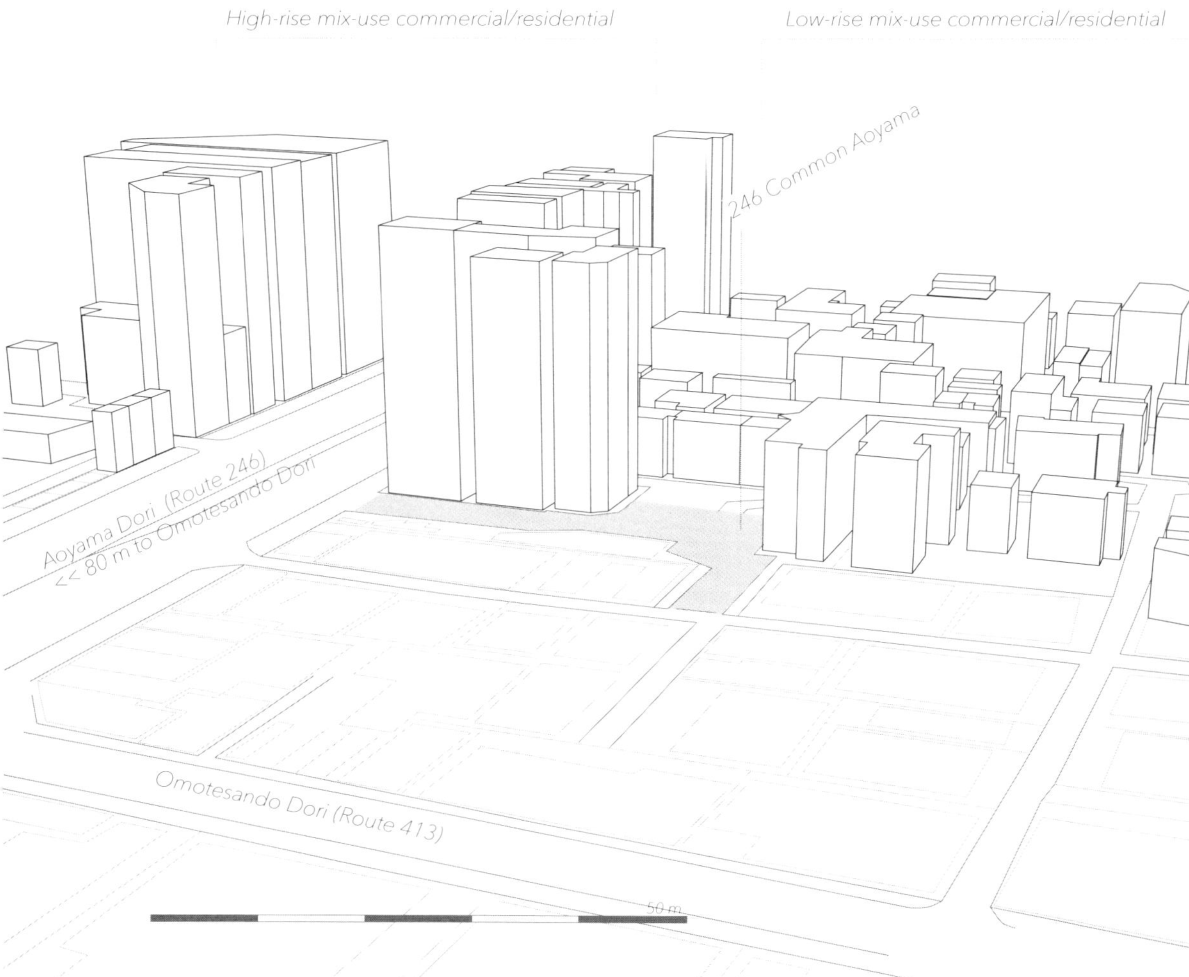

Omotesando Street, a tree-lined boulevard featuring fashion boutique designed by star architects, connects Yoyogi park and Meiji Shrine with the expensive Aoyama neighborhood. Route 246, part of Tokyo's metropolitan ring road, cuts through the area with an edge of ten- to twelve-story commercial buildings. In contrast, a small scale mazelike pattern of backstreets defines the district of subculture fashion in Harajuku and high fashion in Aoyama. Countless wedding venues, beauty salons, cafes, and restaurants form attractions for Tokyoites and visitors alike who stroll the narrow backstreets on weekend afternoons.

Pop-up bar at 246 Common

The small scale of two-story commercial and residential buildings in the backstreets, a pronounced topography, and a relatively large amount of mature trees—in gardens and as street trees—create an intimate and quiet atmosphere that invites exploration. Galleries and shops work with the mazelike streets and often don't reveal their location on maps, making discovery part of the experience for consumers, who share their finds on social media websites. In this context, pop-up cafes and galleries occupying vacant spaces, is rarely surprising. Rather, it underlines an undeniable commercialization of public open space culture.

The group of partners involved in this project is also interesting, ranging from an outdoor equipment company for camping and hiking to an organization of carpenters, a think tank, and an organization focusing on the restoration of traditional Japanese *Minka* houses. More than just simple sponsors, these partners represent a group of like-minded individuals and businesses that share similar cultural and social values. In this aspect, 246 Common is certainly different from the occasional temporary food stalls that pop up in fashionable districts such as Shibuya or Shimokitazawa. With its eco-consciousness, community values, appreciation of the beauty of Japanese products and culture, the project also suggests possibilities for how this and similar projects may be taken further.

A far cry from the subtle activities of the Tokyo Picnic Club or the sustainable agenda of the farmers' markets is the Wildmagic Outdoor Park in Toyosu. Covering a 1.6-hectare area on a former industrial site in Tokyo Bay, this project is all about vastness, offering one of the rare places in Tokyo where people can enjoy openness and the city's skyline—including the Tokyo Tower to the west and Tokyo Sky Tree to the north. Against this background of vast open space, it is not surprising that the organizers create an image for the project that refers to the America Midwest as the land of the big sky and endless opportunities. The program reflects this image and offers an "Americanized" version of outdoor recreation in all its stereotypical facets, including: high-end barbeque facilities, a barbeque restaurant offering a hearty menu with the classic rump steak, car parking next to the picnic spots, silver caravans, and container studio spaces. Cacti and country-style artifacts complete the image visually.

Essentially, the Wildmagic Urban Outdoor Park is a highly commercialized space, where the party- and consumption-oriented crowds can immerse in the instantaneous, the here and now. The facilities are particularly appealing to large family gatherings and to high school and university student groups who can enjoy, relax and "go wild" for a few hours. Initially, the site was only leased from 2012–2013, but the project has proven so successful that it will continue. As such, this project fits perfectly with Ophuis' remarks about consumer space, weekend urbanism, and eventification. Here, we can observe a cosmopolitan understanding of open space by the younger generation based on Western concepts. In contrast to conventional open space typologies with immense restrictions, the project promotes a changing demand for outdoor spaces that encourage play and activity—not just passive recreation.

Although the slogan "Changing the world for a better future,"[22] which summarizes the bigger ideas of this project, seems highly exaggerated and the entire setup of this space is a bit superficial, there is nonetheless an interesting point in all this: essentially, the project suggests a changing attitude towards the urban outdoors. People suddenly like being outside, not only during the few weeks of pleasant weather in spring and autumn.

Outdoor activities now extend into the hot and humid summer months and a barbeque is nowadays even possible in the middle of the winter. And while Wildmagic is far from the fascination of the "real outdoors,"[23] it still points to a new appreciation of roughness, dirtiness, and the incomplete that come with the exposure to the elements.

While Tokyo's pop-up spaces are predominantly organized by younger people, who have experienced the growing number of temporary activities overseas and want to establish something similar at home, older people seem absent, if not disconnected, from these events. Elderly people turn to more traditional ways of informal outdoor activities—e.g., flowerpot gardening. This leads us to the question of how viable these practices are in the future and whether they will fulfill the demands of coming generations? Can the creative practices that have emerged in recent years on vacant land even change the way Tokyo's public space is perceived? Evidently, a large number of parks in Tokyo today are not only inadequately designed to address demand or to create a desire for usage, but overemphasized regulations also prevent creative expression and play. Too often, they also extrude an aura of unattractiveness and blandness that can only be associated with paralysis. The examples above, however demonstrate that vacant spaces, with their spatial and material quality of imperfection, inspire—at least occasionally—activity and progress. In addition, Japan's food fetish and eco-fashion, an awareness for organic food production, and a renewed interest in locally grown produce—supported by a government campaign that aims to raise Japan's food self-sufficiency[24]—certainly provide a platform for not only the farmers' markets. We may also see more productive use of vacant land in the future.

Wildmagic

Toyosu, Minato-ku, Tokyo, Japan

Type:	*vacant development plot*
Ownership:	*private*
Use:	*commercial use, pop-up cafe, bar and rental BBQ*
Size:	*approx. 1.6 ha*
Duration:	*2012–2015*

The temporary commercial project opens the large post-industrial site in Toyosu to Tokyoites in search of barbeque and camping fun. Containers frame the site and offer a range of services ranging from food stalls to entertainment programs. Individual sites including barbeque facilities and equipment can be rented on an hourly basis. Overnight camping is neither intended or allowed. Wildmagic fills a niche that offers "managed" dirt and adventure, while suggesting ideas of freedom and a great view of Tokyo's skyline. While the project is immensely successful, it points to a lack of open spaces that allow active engagement with the environment. In summer 2014 a new "beach resort" addtion and a substantially enlarged BBQ site underline the sucess of this project.

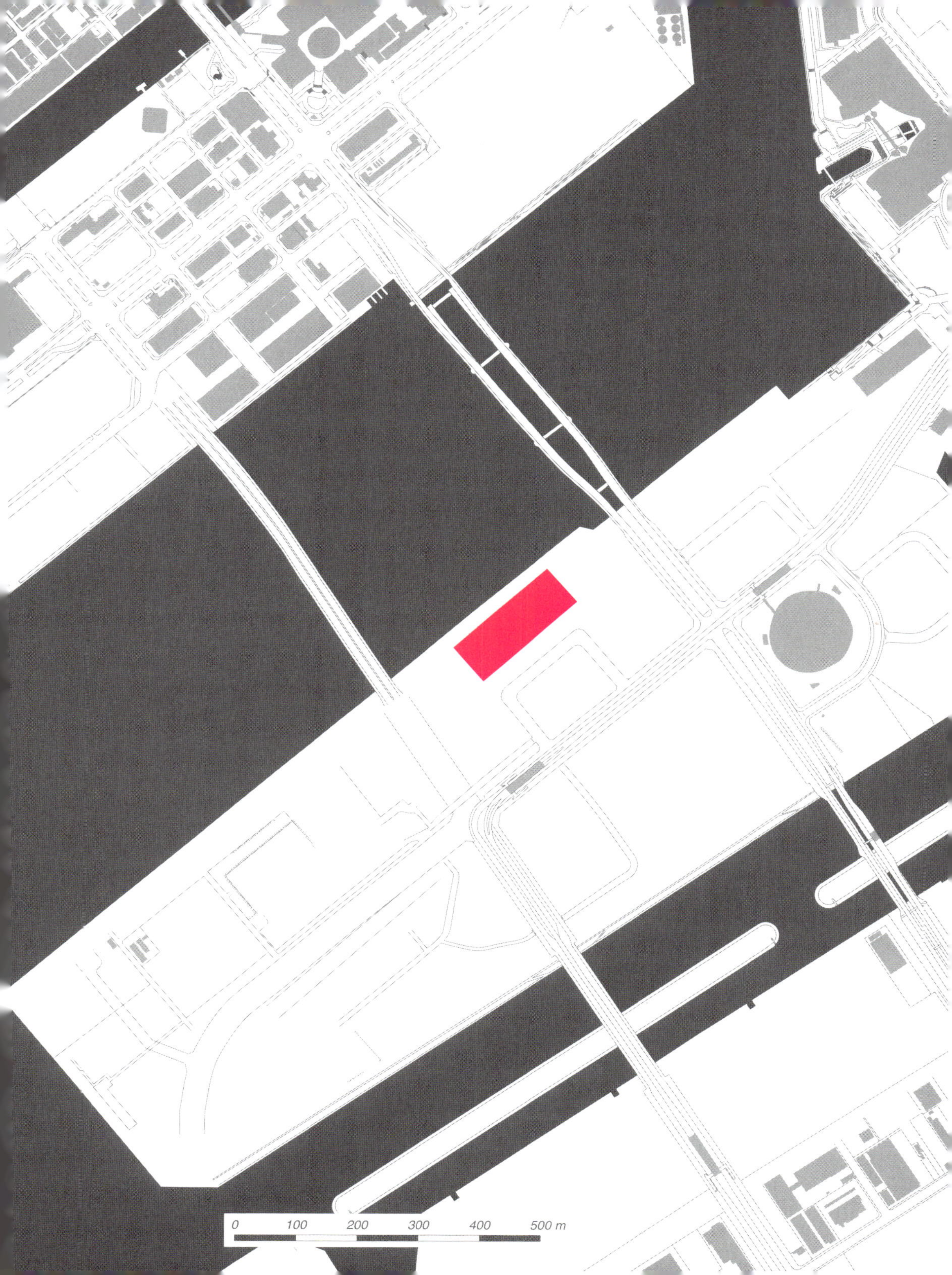
0
100
200
300
400
500 m

Wildmagic, Toyosu, Tokyo, 2013

Rental BBQ, food van, at Wildmagic, Toyosu, Tokyo, 2012

CHAPTER 2

Matter & Materiality

Tokyo resembles the unstructured forms of the rainforest, within which there is in fact many types of creatures co-existing, whilst each constructing their own world. This is ecology, which understands the creature itself in relation to its living environment. If we stop using the metaphors of mechanistics [sic] and semiology and start using the metaphor of ecology, then it should be possible to discover layer upon layer of meaningful environmental unities, even within the landscape of Tokyo.

Atelier Bow-Wow[1]

Urban voids can perform as live spaces and in creative experiments. Tokyo's voids are appropriated for domestic uses and used as parking spaces. Shifting the focus, we realize that urban voids equally perform in their own right through materiality, atmospheres, and through absence of anthropogenic alteration. Contextualized in an idea of inwardness, performative aspects of Tokyo's urban voids will be discussed by investigating a material ecology in ground, atmospheres, and vegetation.

Oku is a spatial term used to describe centripetal inwardness, a traditional Japanese concept of spatial formation.[2] Unlike Western models of a focused centralization, Japanese cities, buildings, gardens, shrines, and everyday objects—such as Kimonos—are traditionally based on inwardness. Oku literally translates to "the innermost," which lies at the core of a space and is organized into multiple layers, similar to an onion, giving depth to a bounded area. Often, the innermost is not revealed, as in shrines where the inner area is off limits and can only be viewed from a distance. After the journey through a series of delineated spaces this nonaccessible *inner* seems to be a quasi-infinite space where a particular scale reveals specific detail in an area that, when enlarged, reveals even more detail and seems infinite on a molecular level. This can be likened to the "Powers of Ten" where each zoom focuses in on more detail, and depth only reveals more detail.

In Japan, a cultural sensitivity has been developed, which is finely attuned to detail; this has often been often linked to a historically long exposure to highly dense living conditions.[3] This ability to focus on detail allows the perception of parts in a finite space. In separating space into parts, smaller entities are created, which manifest the internalization. Therefore, internalization is not a mere reaction to preexisting conditions, but becomes a strategic tool for structuring urban form.

One result of the focus on inwardly oriented detail can be seen in the seemingly chaotic fragmentation of Tokyo's urban form, where each individual building is considered, yet a cohesive structure is not achieved. The highly dynamic and fragmented nature of most of Tokyo's urban fabric stands in stark contrast to the unified spatial experience often presented quite effortlessly by Western cities. Unlike them, Tokyo is chaotic. Donald Ritchie likens Tokyo's spatial structure to a box of spilled toys[4]; each individual toy is carefully designed,

Ground Materiality
Urban Void, Kitazawa
Setagaya-ku, 2012

but bears no relation to others or to their contexts. The individuality of buildings reflects the pattern of individual lots, where walls don't connect: a paradox in one of the world's densest urban environments. Thomas Daniell poignantly states: "Perhaps the central paradox of Japanese architecture is that a cityscape of such incredible heterogeneity is produced by an apparently conformist society. The tiny lots and constant replacement of building stock act to reduce architecture's wider social and urban responsibilities, vindicating the most perverse and indulgent designs."[5]

By understanding urban voids as inwardly oriented and deeply detailed spaces rather than interchangeable volumes, these spaces offer the possibility to trace a quasi-infinite and inwardly oriented nature of Tokyo. Consequently, a landscape pattern of deep qualities emerges that can be traced through the materiality of Tokyo's voids, where matter, atmospheric qualities, and materiality perform as devices for reading an infinite inwardness.

Ground

Urban voids essentially manifest themselves as ground. What might be considered ***void*** is the volume hovering above ground, a levitated absence. Ground, though, possesses depth.

Tokyo's voids are mostly clean. They appear kempt. If plants take over, they would not be noticed by passers-by due to immaculate white walls and fences. Only vacant spaces in more dilapidated areas may be exposed and attract rubbish; in residential neighborhoods, occasional litter is usually removed by residents, who are eager to maintain the visual integrity of their environments by sweeping fallen leaves and collecting rubbish. The desire to maintain a clear order is expressed through the practice of clearing vacant lots of vegetation and debris, covering the ground to keep new vegetation in check, or by the more lucrative practice of turning the vacant space into a clean bitumen-surfaced car park. Larger voids are rarely noticeable, masked to blend into the building fabric by tall, immaculate walls mimicking frontages and the spatial attributes of buildings. The largest tracts of vacant land are inaccessible, surrounded by fences endlessly displaying the ubiquitous slogan: *anzen dai ichi*—safety first. Road readjustment produces spatial expressions that defy the bizarre: cage-like structures of green fences in the middle of sidewalks, empty no-access areas in centers of activity.

The processes of urban transformation and reconfiguration leave voids in distinct states. The materiality of the ground surface ranges from open soil to bitumen, concrete, tiles, gravel, remnant vegetation, and accumulated debris of building material. Often a combination of more than one material determines the ground surface of the void, and in most cases the ground surface material of the previous building is left on the site. Layered surface materials such as floor tiles, which become abandoned and exposed to natural forces, erode and accumulate dirt and vegetation. A temporary fixing of a new ground material and buildup of neostrata occurs. This "authentic nature"[6] stands as a stark contrast to the surrounding immaculate surfaces in the urban context.

Building remnants—such as floor tiles, drains, pavement, and wall foundations—remain as traces of building sites, revealing past programs and functions. A narrow row of stepping stones next to remains of a tiled bathroom floor might indicate an entry space to a bar, whereas larger tiles and rooms indicate retail and production of fresh food. Footprints of buildings remain largely intact in areas cleared for land readjustment processes. Other remnants are paving stones used in alleyways of *nagaya* row houses. The nagaya row houses have disappeared, yet the footprint of the alley remains. These granite paving stones are often historic relicts of the Edo period. Surface materiality has the ability to transform the programmatic capacity of voids. For instance, the act of leveling and cleaning the site of building remnants and urban detritus and sealing its surface using standard materials and techniques blurs the boundary of urban void and programmed space. Urban voids left with sealed bitumen and semisealed gravel surfaces attract uses including car parks and pop-up food stalls, as discussed previously.

Urban voids expose the ground material as remnants of destructive events. Territorial fragments of eroded ground surfaces and decontextualized programs remake ground in images of ruptures. These ruptures do not result from absence but from what is left. But maybe the expectation of an undisturbed continuous urban surface is what is destructive? Processes of growth, change, decay, and stagnation exist within the urban condition. The traces of a material past and the accumulation of an authentic nature might be seen as another layer in the buildup of a rich stratum of the city. "Unrecognizable in its original form … debris signifies not only the return of society to nature but exists as a type of latent hybrid nature in its own right."[7] Voids might be seen as existing as latent hybrid nature in their own right, as they are equally unrecognizable to their original form and continue evolve as spaces of uncontrolled material processes.

Urban voids expose dirt. Ground matter, open soil is a rare material in Tokyo, where an estimated 89 percent[8] of the urban surface area is sealed. Open soil has absorptive and accumulative capacities and performs as a growth medium. Unsealed surfaces absorb liquids and air depending on soil type, degree of compaction, as well as height of the groundwater table. Locally absorbed rainwater feeds back into local aquifers, because it is not drained through a drainage system. This capacity can help to mitigate storm surge events and contribute to the building of water resources. Moist ground can contribute to evaporation and cooling effects in a local microclimate. The effectiveness of rainwater absorption and localized cooling is increased by ground cover vegetation that helps to keep the ground porous and rich in organic matter. Naturally, open soil attracts spontaneous vegetation. In contrast, solid surface materials—such as bitumen or concrete—perform distinctly, by accumulating or directing rainfall water runoff and providing level stability, and are often uniform in their appearance.

A direct relationship between a capacity for absorption and urban voids is exposed in relation to pollutants—such as chemicals from the residue of

Reflected space
Urban Void, Yanaka, Bunkyo-ku, 2012

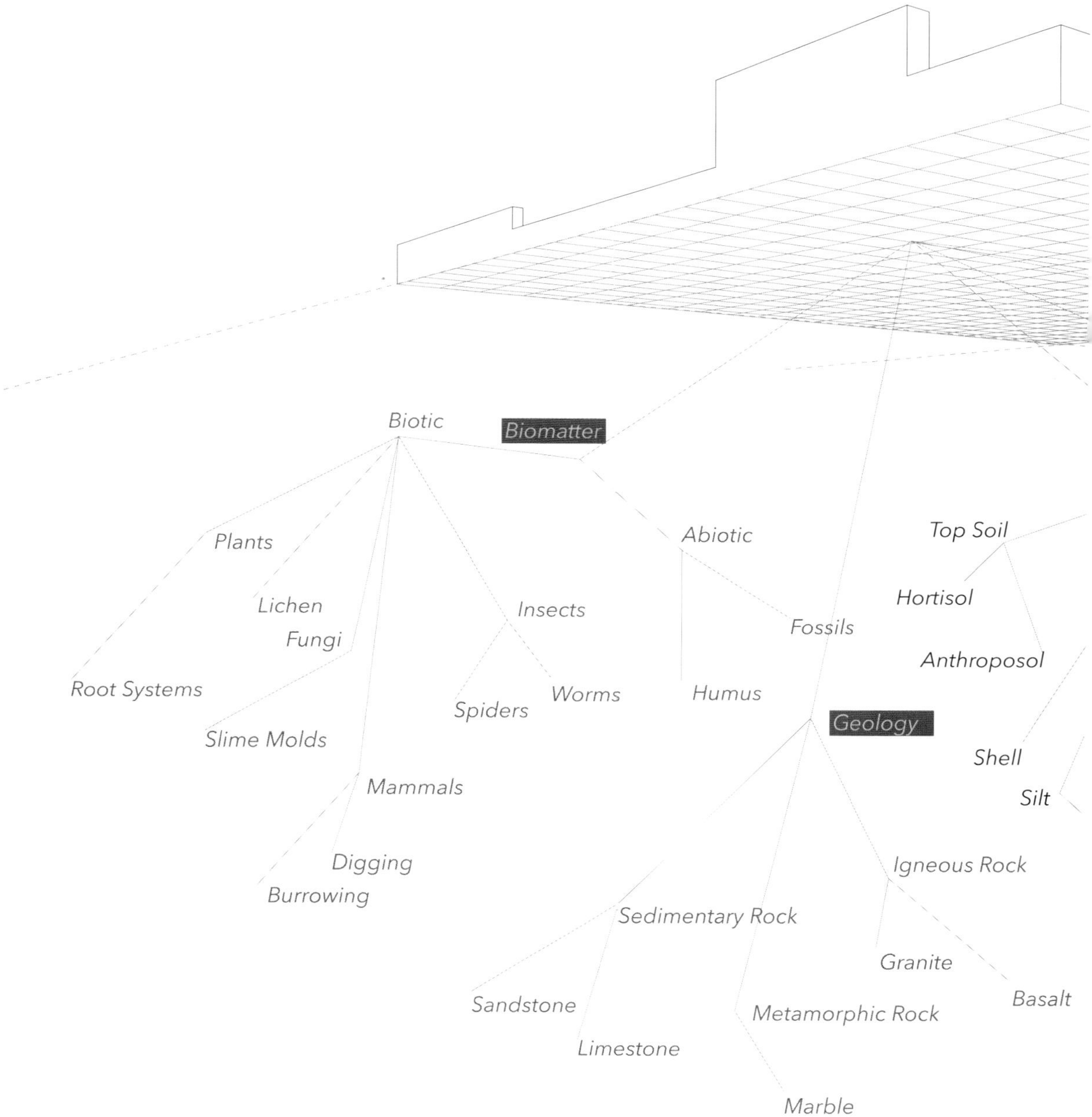

Ground contains, filters, stores, and transports material, water, air. The foundations of cities sustain, stabilize, erode, and collapse. A treacherous stability is exemplified in Tokyo where roughly 1,000 earthquakes occur each year.
Tokyo's urban voids expose the surface layer of the city's foundations: invisible strata of soils, specific to site and context, infrastructure, and accumulated traces.

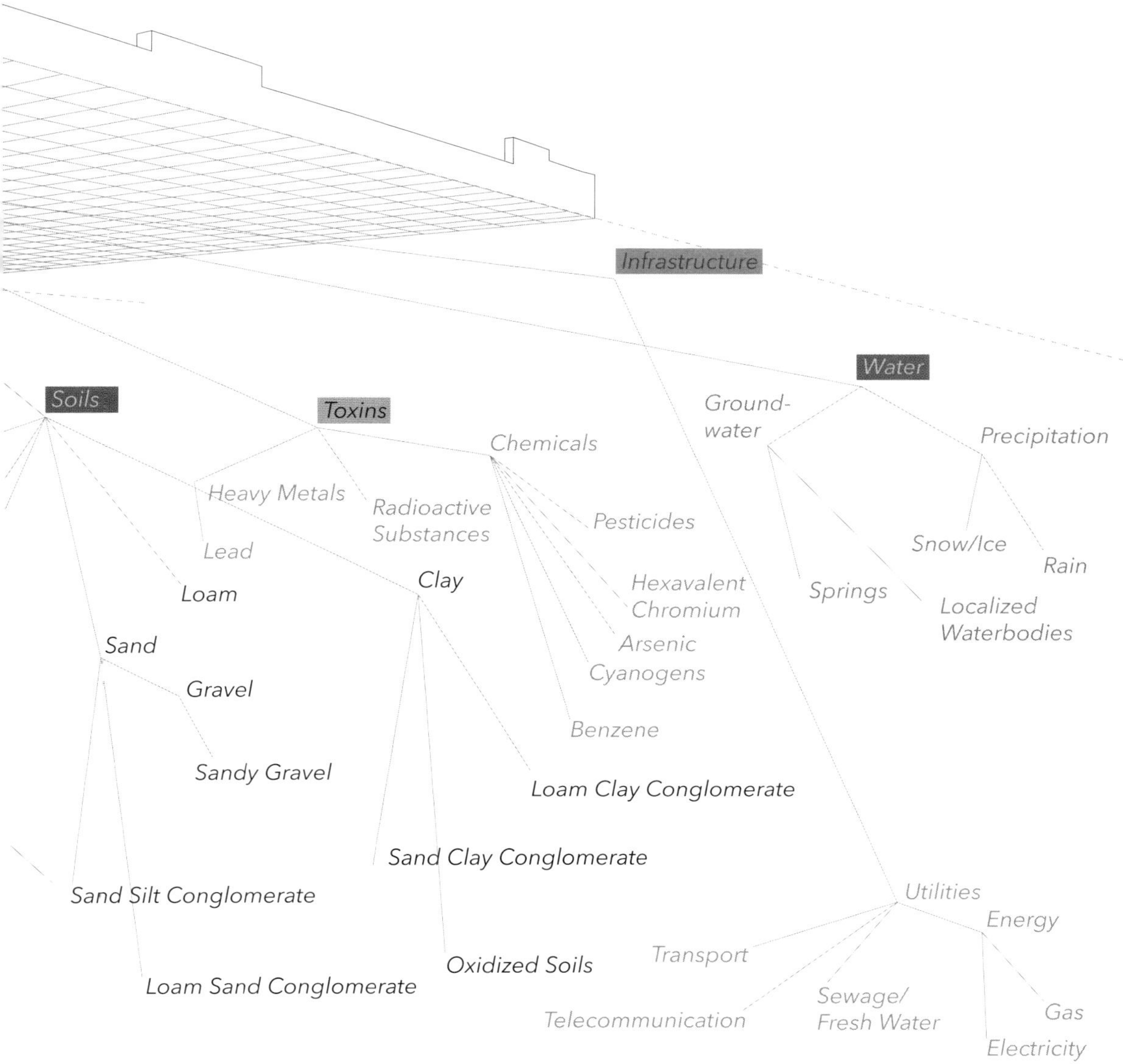

Soils, geology, water, and toxin data relate to Tokyo's specific conditions and have been retrieved from Tokyo Metropolitan Government documents and sites.

pesticides, industrial uses, and radioactive substances. In July 2002, Tokyo Gas and the Tokyo Metropolitan Government concluded an agreement for the relocation of the Tokyo Wholesale Market—including Tsukiji fish market—to Toyosu, one of the islands of reclaimed land in Tokyo Bay. Until 1988, a Tokyo Gas processing and production plant operated on the site, which left the site highly contaminated: high levels of lead, arsenic, hexavalent chromium, cyanogens, and benzene were absorbed in the groundwater and soil. Some of the toxins were released into the atmosphere during the 2011 Great East Japan Earthquake.[9] The cost for a joint effort to replace, purify, and stabilize the soil to a depth of 4.5 meters and cover the surface with concrete and asphalt was approximated in 2011 at 7.8 billion yen,[10] and exceeded 10.43 billion yen in late 2013.[11] The extensive remediation processes are all executed on-site in processing plants and airtight tents, and include extensive groundwater treatment and sealing of the site to prevent further ground- and seawater pollution. The soil decontamination process includes deep excavation, microbial treatment, medium heat temperature treatment, and washing.[12] However, it remains a matter of public debate whether the heavy contamination can be fully resolved to allow a safe handling of fresh food on the future market site.[13] In addition, increased construction and labor costs have led to further delays; in late 2013, the Tokyo Metropolitan Government failed to find builders for the market facilities worth 63 billion yen.[14]

Anthrosols are soils that have been formed or altered by human cultivation or land manipulation processes, such as terracing, draining, and irrigation. The terminology has been mainly related to cultivation processes, however the immense influence of human inhabitation is visible in the composition of ground matter in Tokyo. Sections of Tokyo's soil profile reveal top layers between 0.5–3 meters of soil, which are classified as anthrosol; in the areas of land reclamation, depths range up eighty meters. Viewed from an aerial perspective, Tokyo's artificial islands remain clearly legible as a constructed landscape. Yet from a ground perspective, not all reclaimed land remains readable in that manner, as the reclamation proceeds further out into the bay and older areas become absorbed into the urban context. The 2011 Great East Japan Earthquake caused liquefaction in large parts of the reclaimed lands, which resulted in severe damage to 3,800 buildings and infrastructure. One of the most severely damaged areas, Urayasu in Chiba prefecture, was constructed in the nineteen-sixties by pumping dredged sand from Tokyo Bay into what would become the newly reclaimed area. In 2011, sand eruptions of gray silt flooded the streets of Urayasu, bringing the foundation material of the suburb to the surface, in a neighborhood not immediately recognizable as reclaimed.

Ground performs as recorder of human and seismic activities by its capacity to absorb and accumulate material residue, and demonstrates that previous uses can reverberate over long periods of time while they remain unseen. Part of a system, flows transport accumulated matter and manifest events through layers of time in soil horizons.

Tokyo is a topographic city. Its geomorphology—the Musahino highland plateau, the alluvial plains of the river estuary of Sumidagawa, and the Arakawa and Edogawa rivers—determines its contemporary urban form. Large-scale landform manipulation in artificial islands, canals, and moats is part of Tokyo's history. In the Edo period, rerouting of rivers and land reclamation transformed wide areas of the low-lying lands into a water city of canals. The filling of one of the first large-scale land reclamation areas, Hibiya inlet near Imperial Palace, was completed in 1592. In contemporary Tokyo, sophisticated flood control systems—including dams, seawalls, drain channels, and flood control sluices—are in place in the low-lying areas. In some places, the alluvial soil profile deep in the ground remains one of the few tangible indicators of an estuary landscape.

Traditionally, Tokyo's land use has been related to topography. During the feudal system of the Edo period (1603–1868), two distinct urban conditions of *Yamanote* and *Shitamachi* emerged. In the center of Edo, the Shogun castle (present-day Imperial Palace) was located on the headland of the Musashino plateau. The highland, the Yamanote (mountain hand) extends in seven main ridges towards the west, and historically is also referred to as "the city of fields and gardens."[15] Yamanote was traditionally home to the upper class; the samurai and daimyo estates were found there. The lower classes lived in the dense Shitamachi (low town), which formed in the lowlands along rivers and canals of Edo, as "the city of water." As a result of the urban structure shaped by topography, parts of Shitamachi existed within the valleys of Yamanote. Plot size and form in the Yamanote and Shitamachi areas differed significantly: large irregular plots with gardens in the highlands and gridded small plots in the low areas. South-facing slopes were used as terraced faming grounds.

Hajime Ishikawa describes an "invisibility of the ground and the ghost of topography," and contends that Tokyo's building morphology holds topographical patterns that remain hidden in the dense urban fabric.[16] Terraced building plots cut into slopes erase irregular inclines from the urban topography. There the urban topography can be traced through water and drainage systems inside buildings that effectively operate as mini-catchments. The new *mosaic topography* of terraced plots is manifested in 3D digital maps.[17]

Tokyo's urban voids expose the ghosts of topography. Fragments of terrace structures, walls, soil strata, and traces of building floor plates on adjacent building walls become visible in open sites. Remnant building structures blur the boundaries of the ground and reveal how Tokyo extends in and above ground level. Topography, buildup of ground material in anthropogenic strata, and the resulting landform link to larger systematic connections: where urban voids are seen in isolation, a deeper investigation of the ground plane erases property boundaries and other superficial demarcations.

An understanding of deepness might allow for new readings of urban ecosystems and question the notion of the ground being a place to bury and hide the unwanted.

Connecting ground and voids produces depth in relational aspects, such as the material capacity of the ground in absorption and buildup of strata; gives readings to topography through traces that would remain invisible; and opens up possibilities to think deeply about vacancy as a concept and question the notion of emptiness.

Atmospheres/Presence

Nothing is harder, yet nothing is more necessary, than to speak of certain things whose existence is neither demonstrable nor probable. The very fact that serious and conscientious men treat them as existing things brings them a step closer to existence and to the possibility of being born.

Hermann Hesse[18]

Urban voids offer a range of atmospheric projections: qualitative spatial meanings as well as material and performative readings. Yet, to discuss the performance of what might essentially be nothing is a paradox. The question is how can absence be described as presence? A material ground offers the first reading; the atmospheric volume the second.

Atmospheres can be discussed in qualitative terms, a notion that is widely associated with voids, perceived as a strange otherness.[19] The meanings associated with the term "vacancy" suggest stagnation, a negative other, untamed, chaotic aspect that is best hidden behind walls to maintain integrity. The presence of voids has been described as intimidating and negative.[20] Voids have been seen as the other nature that liberates us from a predetermined existence.[21] We have described it as a space that goes further to offer possibilities through its very imperfect nature. The void tears a hole in the surface of a city, which is expected to perform through predetermined functions, and the unfamiliarity of the unused is baffling, inviting. By assigning meanings, the attempt is being made to somehow fill it, to make use of it.

Atmospheres can as well be described through experiential terms: the damp, dark, closed; the open, windy, exposed. Atmospheres allow bodily perceptions, sensations, and experiences: the smell of wet soil shortly before or after rain, the sound of dripping water, an expansive horizon. This experiential notion crosses over to a qualitative reading of voids where these spaces perform as the Other, as contrasting medium. As David Gissen describes in *Subnature* these spaces produce, form, and accumulate alternative ecologies that occupy these spaces.

Atmosphere
Urban Void, Kita-ku, 2012

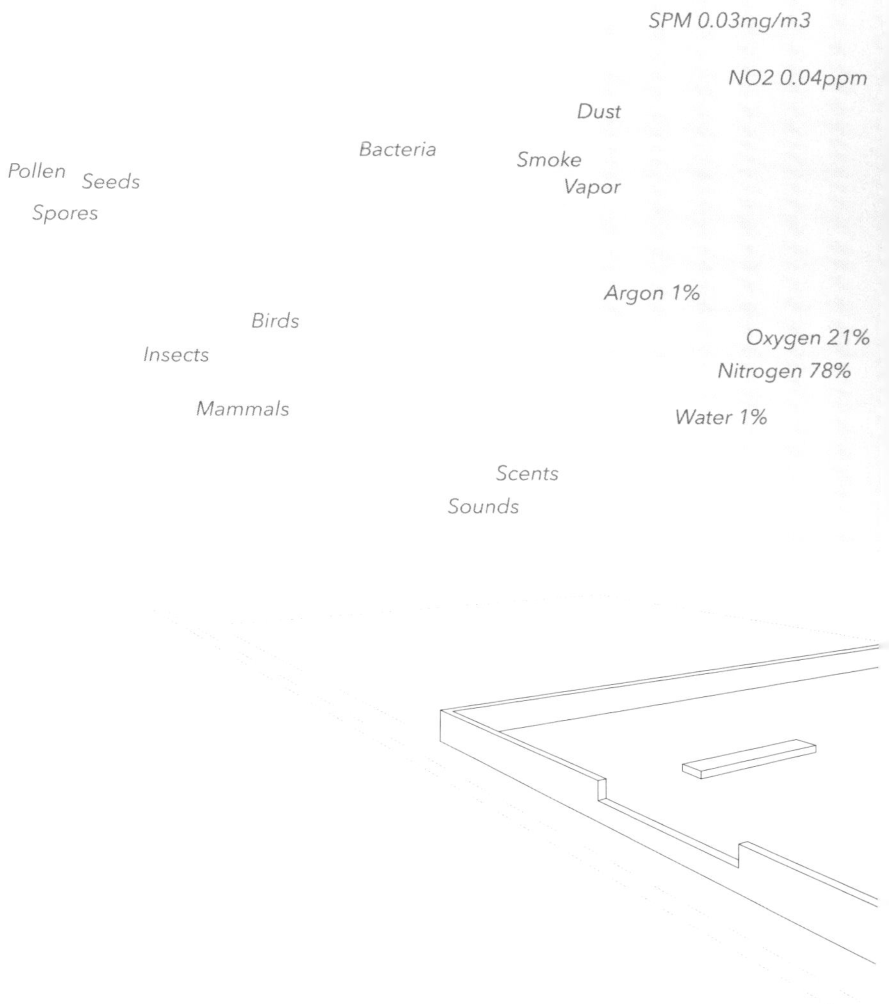

The atmospheric and climatic aspects of space are exemplified in treating void as volume: where microscopic matter makes up air, flows of air create movement. Void is not empty. The invisible aspects of the volumetric space define its presence. The relationship between ground, surface, material context, and air define the void volume on micro scale.

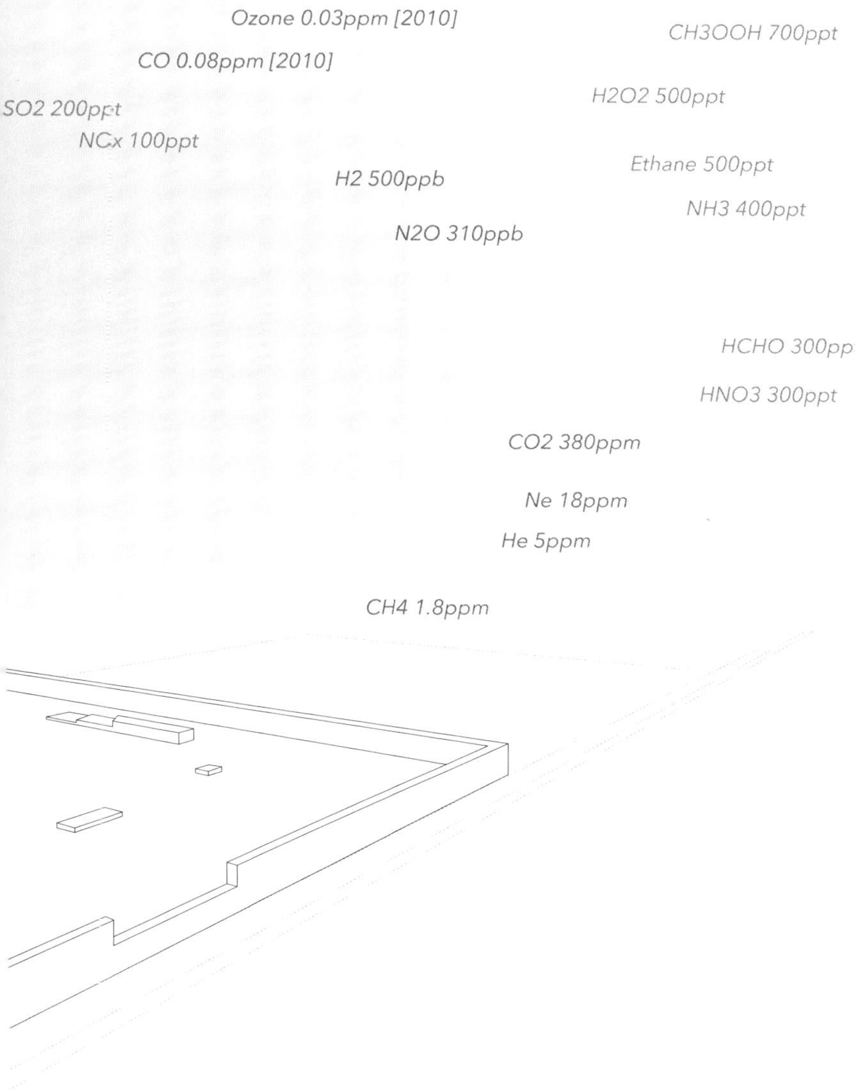

All data relate to Tokyo's specific conditions and have been retrieved from Tokyo Metropolitan Government documents and sites.

Atmospheres of dust and oily fumes, dripping from exhaust fans into abandoned spaces. Roaches and weeds colonize the dampness; Others, bland and uninteresting, nonperforming, not in poetic or pragmatic terms.[22]

Voids can be essentially seen as volumes of air: a flowing, ever-present invisible entity that connects and transports sounds and scent, and contains a wide range of microscopic particles, chemicals, water, and dust. Air can be stale, humid, cold, in motion, form clouds and fog, and is maybe the closest reminder to a transcendent nature we can perceive—if we perceive it. It is important to note that air, as we know it, is regulated: air conditioning systems define indoor spaces as distinct from outside spaces; a thermic boundary is created by the ubiquitous infrastructure. Constant set temperatures and humidity, and the absence of air movement, are characteristic for inside spaces. Air is filtered, cooled, or heated; the outside air functions as a resource for interior space. Air as nature is uncontrolled and relative.

In considering the aspects of air and atmospheres as ephemeral sensations, connected in flows and with the capacity for relational readings, it becomes clear that voids are naturally spaces with the capacity for forming and contributing to urban microclimates. In Tokyo's urban context of extreme building density, sealed surfaces, and blocked wind flows, specific meso- and microclimates can be observed. One specific expression of Tokyo's urban climate is the forming of urban heat islands in areas of central Tokyo. During hot summer days, reduced wind flows, heat absorbed in building materials, and heat emissions through building systems and automobiles cause the formation of heat islands—areas of intense and prolonged heat. These extreme climatic phenomena are caused by combination of factors: urban form and materiality, availability of urban green for evapotranspiration, additional heat sources such as traffic and air-conditioning units, and the availability of wind flows. In understanding a complex and multicausal condition, it is evident that possible solutions need to address multiple aspects to be effective.

Extreme heat waves in the early 2000s led the Tokyo Metropolitan Government to implement a set of guidelines with the aim to control heat islands. The use of heat environment maps is required for building permissions, and a "Tokyo Model" of control measures is to be implemented. Suggested countermeasures specific to each area and urban structure type include: greening of the building area, and where possible, rooftop greening, greening of building walls; reflective material on rooftops; water-retentive pavements; and the reduction of artificial pavements and anthropogenic waste heat.[23]

On the small scale, the climatic conditions of urban voids can be investigated similarly: a combination of surface cover and material, degree of exposure and enclosure form distinct conditions for site-specific microclimates. Predominant types of urban voids in Tokyo are vacant plots that read as gaps between buildings, empty lots in less dense areas that are clearly

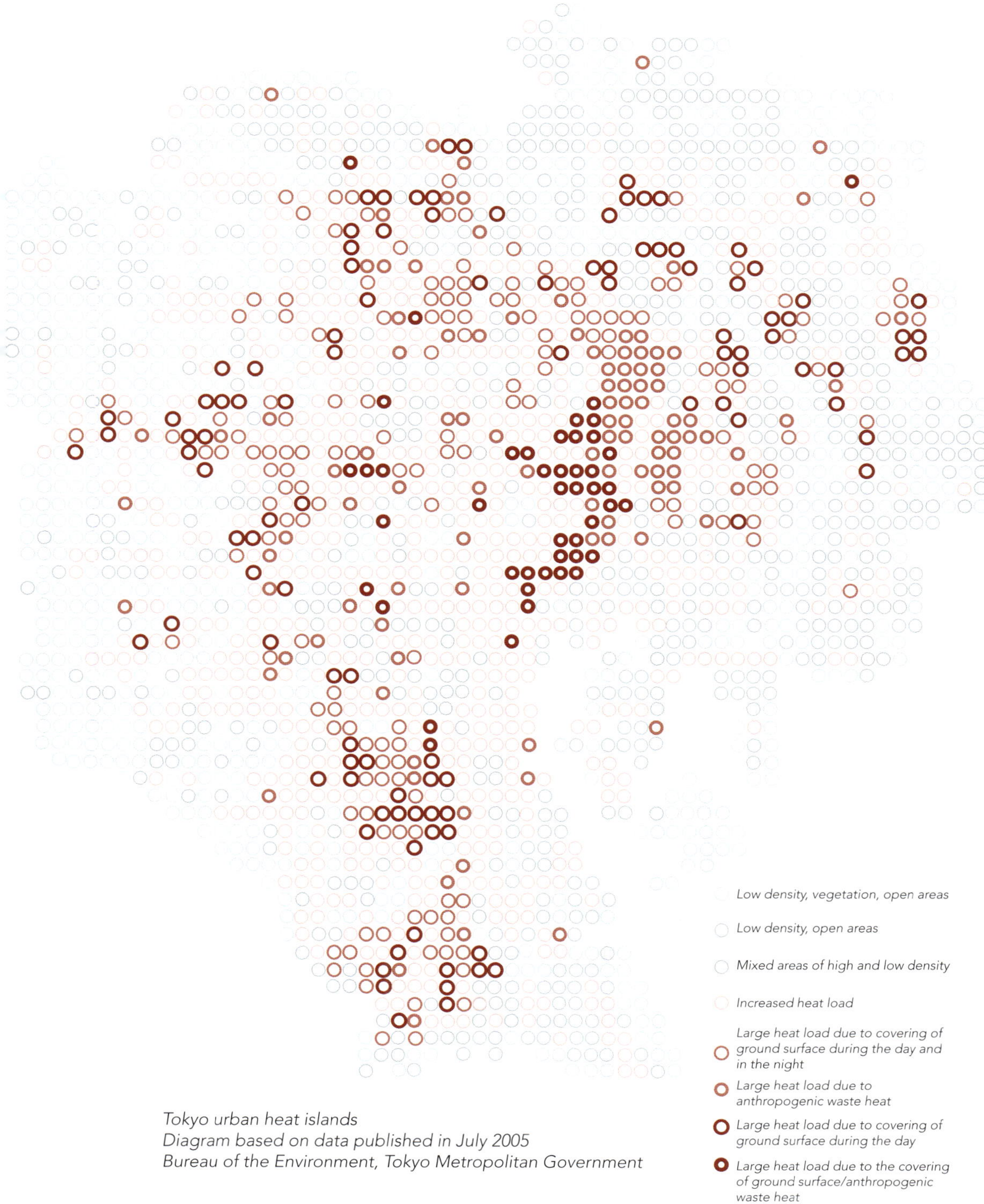

Tokyo urban heat islands
Diagram based on data published in July 2005
Bureau of the Environment, Tokyo Metropolitan Government

Atmosphere
Urban Void, Taito-ku, 2013

visible as building plots, multiple voids in road readjustment areas that form corridors, and large tracts of vacant lands in land reclamation sites. The gap voids are characterized by a high degree of enclosure by usually tall surrounding buildings that cause overshadowing, resulting in darkness and dampness. Types characterized as empty plots occur in areas with low-rise and less dense building structures with one to two stories and small gardens. There, microclimates are strongly dependent on ground surface material, vegetation, and exposure. Linear voids, such as those emerging through road readjustment projects, form channel-like conditions that can contribute to increased permeability and airflow. Large open voids—like those found in Toyosu and Kita-ku—can contribute to increased evapotranspiration through their vegetation and open soil, and allow for airflows.

Considering atmospheric qualities and identifying the presence of air, it becomes apparent that absence is caught in the meaning and perspective on voids. Seeing voids as entities performing in their own right as parts of a system in urban ecology brings out the richness of microclimates, which are relative to each site, and allows us to see the connection between ground, context, and air achieved in these spaces.

Vegetation

Spontaneous vegetation—in the form of grasses, escaped garden plants, and tree seedlings—are subtly defining a pattern of Tokyo's urban ecosystem. Weeds colonize the void spaces in the metropolis, where they disrupt the inherent urban order on a micro scale. These micro natures can serve to form a landscape pattern that maps human interference, or rather, noninterference. David Gissen describes weeds as useless plants, "forces against the established forms of social order."[24] The wild debris of nature, weeds take over the nonplaces of the city. They thrive in the smallest spaces, they grow in cracks, behind fences, in dark and inaccessible spaces—and colonize voids anywhere and in any city.

However, in Tokyo—where effective use of space is defined by "impossible" buildings,[25] and the famous infrastructure tangles of elevated expressways, shopping centers, and golf course cages[26]—every centimeter of city space is used and spontaneous vegetation can almost be considered an endangered species, with the exception of urban voids that function as hotbeds of biodiversity. Describing the conditions under which Tokyo's residual vegetation emerges requires yet another shift in perspective and scale.

Weeds, the same as any other type of spontaneous vegetation, form patterns specific to a space. The pattern produced by weeds can be seen as the translation of site conditions such as: availability of water, sunlight, air, soil type and nutrients, as well as the degree of human interference.

In phytosociology, the study of plant communities, weeds are classified in Neophyta (new plants), species accompanying or depending on human activity. Site conditions such as exposure, soil type and program can be described as exogenic factors influencing a plant, whereas the plant-specific characteristics are viewed as endogenic factors. The endogenic factors include competition between plants, and synergies between plants such as symbiosis. The interactions between plants and the competition for light, nutrients, and space illustrate the complexity in the formation of types of spontaneous vegetation.

The term Neophyta essentially points to the effects of all urbanization processes and the alteration of the so-called natural environment. The gradual development processes and peaks of growths that have made Tokyo one of the largest human settlements on Earth are also responsible for the radical change of the vegetation typically defining the Kanto Plain. The altering of landform, topography, water bodies, and vegetation is closely tied to human inhabitation and settlement, and has a particular history in Tokyo where topography is tied to societies and their strata. In the Edo Period (1603–1868), numerous factors contributed to the formation of a spatially segregated city pattern that reflected the strata of a feudal society. Waley, Ashihara, and Jinnai are among the scholars who have rigorously investigated the relationship between urban form and society, and the resulting effects on contemporary Tokyo through Shitamachi and Yamanote.[27] Hajime Ishikawa, landscape architect and urban researcher, has mapped Tokyo's topography and shown the direct relation between landform and urban form; constructing physical spatial images of Yamanote and Shitamachi as discussed through topography.[28]

While the formation of voids is related to spatial patterns in the urban context as developed through sociopolitical conditions, the vegetation is related to the specific site conditions. Depending primarily on exposure and ground material, Tokyo's urban vacant plots function as various types of localized micro ecosystems: some of them thickly overgrown in vegetation, hidden away from human interference in the smallest laneways of old neighborhoods; some of them large open tracts of unused land waiting for development. Most vacant lots in the inner and low-lying areas—such as Taito (mainly sandy loam soils)—are overshadowed by neighboring buildings, creating dark and damp habitats for predominantly mosses and grasses, whereas the large fields in Toyosu (landfill soils) are dominated by a wide range of sun-loving pioneering species such as Solidago canadensis (Canadian goldenrod). Some vacant lots function as temporary car parks and thus support a distinct type and pattern of vegetation. There, the ground has often been stabilized using a gravel surface and the drier conditions enable a wider range of plants to grow. A few small plots have been undisturbed by human interference and form an impressive habitat for plants, birds, insects, and small mammals.

In these instances, the value of the undisturbed and forgotten becomes evident. French landscape architect Gilles Clement discusses weeds and remnant vegetation in the idea of *jardin planétaire* (the planetary garden), a nondefined leftover space that allows for the existence of weeds and becomes a "biological time capsule" for the future.[29] This "biological time capsule" often maintains a greater biodiversity than the low maintenance, maximum efficiency green provided by municipalities. If we consider the small pockets of Tokyo that have been undisturbed by human interference for years, or in rare cases decades, the potential of this biological time capsule manifests itself in the vegetation. In Yanaka, an area that has been widely discussed in relation to community, authenticity, and density—and which is distinguished by significant topography—a surprising number of small, long-term urban voids are found. In an area of roughly 0.4 square meters, thirteen voids supporting remnant vegetation are found. Their vegetation primarily consists of grasses, bamboo, and various tree seedlings of a dry forest type. These patterns—together with historical records of flora, fauna, topography, watercourses, and inhabitation—can be used to speculate on what an "original" vegetation of the Kanto Plain might look like now if no settlement had occurred; similar to a condition before the arrival of the Tokugawa Shogun in 1603.

The *Mannahatta* project by Eric Sanderson works with these types of data and spatially describes a natural history of New York. In New York, this positioning of the city as an continuous ecosystem has allowed an understanding of a clear link to an inherent dependence on resources that are formed within the highly urbanized context itself: air and water.[30] Tokyo's voids, with their remnant vegetation, have a similar potential: to inform and describe a presettlement condition that allows a closer reading of Tokyo as a complex ecosystem. If voids operate in this system, the vegetation they support can be used to map changes over time, and contexts such as climate extremes. Spontaneous vegetation can operate as a translation device to understand site conditions. Furthermore, fast-growing plants—such as the common reed (Phragmites australis), which frequently occurs on damp vacant sites—produce biomass. Considering this performance aspect, biomass cultivation can be considered another aspect of urban voids. Synergy effects of biomass cultivation, mitigation of urban heat island effects through microclimatic capacities, and the tracing of natural patterns of Tokyo's spontaneous vegetation are possibilities in absence.

Urban voids are inseparably connected to an organic structure of becoming, maturation, and decay. They manifest as bleak illogical emptiness, colonized by patches of spontaneous vegetation, rainwater collecting on an abandoned pavement in puddles, bounded by naked walls reflecting the humming sounds of adjacent air-conditioning units. Tokyo's voids perform in their own right as stark contrast to the modern, vast, metropolis; towering highways and flashing neon lights, shaped by desires, deep from the dark reaches of modernity.

Chrysanthemum spec., Shibuya-ku, 2010

Rubus fruticosus, Chuo-ku, 2011

Dry grass meadow, Chuo-ku, 2010

Solidago canadensis, Chuo-ku, 2011

Solidago canadensis, Chuo-ku, 2011

Chrysanthemum spec., Kita-ku, 2012

Dry grass meadow, Kita-ku, 2011

Leucanthemum spec., Bunkyo-ku, 2011

Dry grass meadow + Rubus spec., Kita-ku, 2012

Dry grass meadow + Rubus spec., Kita-ku, 2012

Sasa spec., Bunkyo-ku, 2012

Polygonum spec., Chuo-ku, 2012

Voids can be read as poetic transmitters of the ephemeral; as transient atmospheres, vegetated wastelands, containers of existence. What they offer is the possibility for deeper questioning and discoveries, and other nonproductive activities and experiences that are unplanned and momentary. In focusing on ephemeral qualities and performative capacities of atmospheres and materiality, recognition for the shifting of scale becomes perceptible. Inwardly, oriented qualities are observed on a detailed scale and become translated to inform a boarder, networked scale. Similarly, a shift in perspective on a specific phenomenon or quality might be translated into a complex and interrelated atmosphere of a site. These shifts are building connections of a material ecosystem.

PART TWO

Tokyo's Spatial Capital

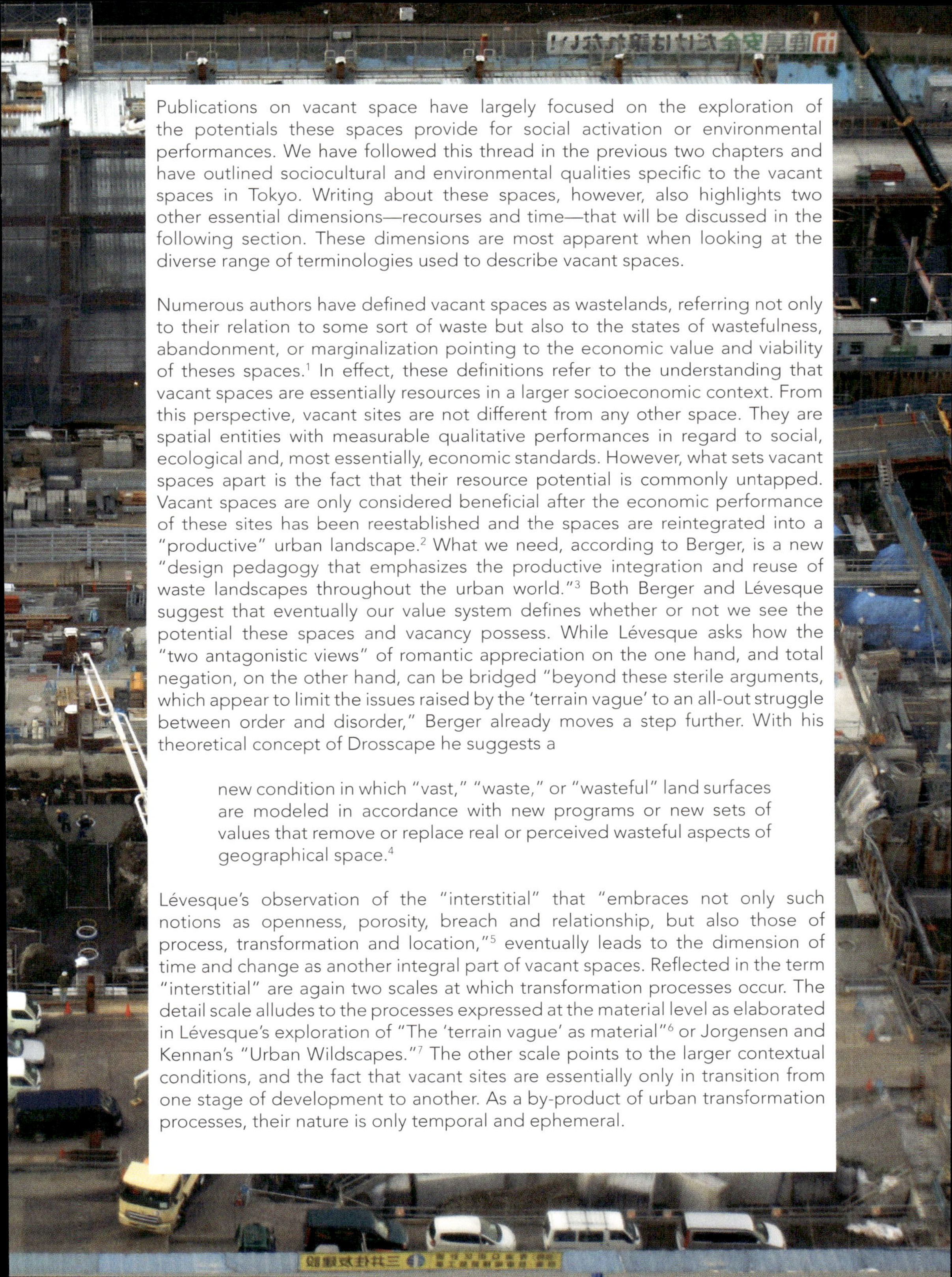

Publications on vacant space have largely focused on the exploration of the potentials these spaces provide for social activation or environmental performances. We have followed this thread in the previous two chapters and have outlined sociocultural and environmental qualities specific to the vacant spaces in Tokyo. Writing about these spaces, however, also highlights two other essential dimensions—recourses and time—that will be discussed in the following section. These dimensions are most apparent when looking at the diverse range of terminologies used to describe vacant spaces.

Numerous authors have defined vacant spaces as wastelands, referring not only to their relation to some sort of waste but also to the states of wastefulness, abandonment, or marginalization pointing to the economic value and viability of theses spaces.[1] In effect, these definitions refer to the understanding that vacant spaces are essentially resources in a larger socioeconomic context. From this perspective, vacant sites are not different from any other space. They are spatial entities with measurable qualitative performances in regard to social, ecological and, most essentially, economic standards. However, what sets vacant spaces apart is the fact that their resource potential is commonly untapped. Vacant spaces are only considered beneficial after the economic performance of these sites has been reestablished and the spaces are reintegrated into a "productive" urban landscape.[2] What we need, according to Berger, is a new "design pedagogy that emphasizes the productive integration and reuse of waste landscapes throughout the urban world."[3] Both Berger and Lévesque suggest that eventually our value system defines whether or not we see the potential these spaces and vacancy possess. While Lévesque asks how the "two antagonistic views" of romantic appreciation on the one hand, and total negation, on the other hand, can be bridged "beyond these sterile arguments, which appear to limit the issues raised by the 'terrain vague' to an all-out struggle between order and disorder," Berger already moves a step further. With his theoretical concept of Drosscape he suggests a

> new condition in which "vast," "waste," or "wasteful" land surfaces are modeled in accordance with new programs or new sets of values that remove or replace real or perceived wasteful aspects of geographical space.[4]

Lévesque's observation of the "interstitial" that "embraces not only such notions as openness, porosity, breach and relationship, but also those of process, transformation and location,"[5] eventually leads to the dimension of time and change as another integral part of vacant spaces. Reflected in the term "interstitial" are again two scales at which transformation processes occur. The detail scale alludes to the processes expressed at the material level as elaborated in Lévesque's exploration of "The 'terrain vague' as material"[6] or Jorgensen and Kennan's "Urban Wildscapes."[7] The other scale points to the larger contextual conditions, and the fact that vacant sites are essentially only in transition from one stage of development to another. As a by-product of urban transformation processes, their nature is only temporal and ephemeral.

The state of flux already briefly appeared in Sola-Morales' definition of terrain vague, as he points to the etymology of the term "vague," which not only includes the meaning of vagueness or otherness, but also relates to a condition fluctuation, instability, and oscillation.[8] In this understanding, most discussions only focus on the transition of the individual site, while in effect, the processes that shape vacant spaces are equally dynamic and change over time. The issue of ephemerality on the larger, urban scale is even more relevant in the Japanese context where urbanism is essentially in itself, as Shelton writes, "flexible," "vague," and "temporary."[9]

Thus, in order to unpack the potential of vacant spaces as a spatial resource, it is necessary to understand the contextual conditions that make the very city in which these spaces are located. Deindustrialization, suburbanization, political regime change, and shrinking population have been assigned to the production of vacancy. The processes are varied and often multilayered. But what are the spatial, economic, and political conditions that form and transform Tokyo and subsequently Tokyo's voids? Certainly, there are elements to theses processes that are comparable with other places around the world. Yet, vacant spaces are produced under very distinct local circumstances, as the transformation processes are essentially context specific. Essentially, each city produces its own set of rules and conditions that allow the temporal ruptures to surface. Berger even states that these spaces "are created and destroyed by processes and values derived from, or because of cultural tastes and actions."[10] As a consequence of these contextual situations, the morphological and typological structures of vacant spaces vary immensely between places. Tokyo's voids are thus in many aspects quite unique—e.g., in their shape, size, ownership, and legislative structure, but also in the aspects of time and flux.

Data used in the next two chapters largely focus on five selected areas, which cover a diverse spectrum of contextual environments. The distinctive demographic, economic, and spatial configurations that shape these neighborhoods and the range of urban transformation processes are reflected in the diversity of vacant space.

東急本店通商店会
中華
本格中華料理
龍盛菜館
2F 宴会
食べ放題
飲み放題
有り
ここ曲り
200m先
3461-8006
円山町
10
通学路
文
吉田医院
スピード落せ

CHAPTER 3

The Politics of Vacancy

It is not only the foreign eye that sees Tokyo as a synonym for extreme urban density and lack of green space.[1] Over the past decade, municipal and local governments have recognized the issues resulting from a lack of urban green space—less than three square meters of open space per capita—but in such a densely built city as Tokyo, it remains difficult to acquire land and invest in open space when there are also pressing demands for other infrastructural facilities. Thus, despite the numerous efforts to increase the amount of green space, the overall figure has remained relatively stable over the past twenty years. In this context, urban voids are an incredible spatial resource in Tokyo, because they have the potential to immediately increase the total amount of open space by 50 percent.[2] But why do voids exactly exist in Tokyo? This chapter explores the economic processes and planning regulations that contribute to the making of vacant spaces and represent a combination of many aspects, including economic decline, political ambitions, urban policy, and tax regulations. The identified processes describe the contextual framework of regulatory and legislative conditions in the Japanese urban context. Other factors are in many aspects quite distinctly tied to the politics and urban issues in Tokyo.

Urban transformation, demographic change, and the particular economic climate of the city all play important roles in the development of vacant space. All of these factors have undergone fundamental changes in the past two decades. Many of the transformation processes, as well as the political and planning decisions discussed below, are tightly connected to the rise and fall of the Japanese economy in the nineteen-eighties and nineteen-nineties. Thus, we cannot discuss the issues related to Tokyo's urban development and the emergence of voids without examining the time of the so-called bubble economy. After a period of rapid economic and urban growth—which started after World War II and peaked during the nineteen-eighties—Japan was hit hard by rapid economic decline caused by the collapse of overinflated land and stock prices. What first looked like a "lost decade" marked by economic recession and stagnation, eventually extended into "lost decades." As W. R. Garside writes, "It is arguable that by the turn of the century it was too soon to know just how long a shadow the experiences of the previous decade had cast."[3] The 2008 global financial crises followed by the 2011 Great East Japan Earthquake marked other big events that negatively impacted Japanese economic performance.

Road readjustment process Shibuya-ku, Higashi Kitazawa, 2011

A single building remains surrounded by cleared and fenced plots for a road readjustment project.

Despite brief moments of recovery, reforms of the country's administrative, economic, and corporate activities have so far proven unsuccessful in spurring significant growth and renewed confidence in the Japanese market. Only in the last year or so with Prime Minister Shinzo Abe's policies, which strongly focus on growth and spending on public works projects, has the economic climate seemingly regained momentum, a development connoted in the term "Abenomics."[4]

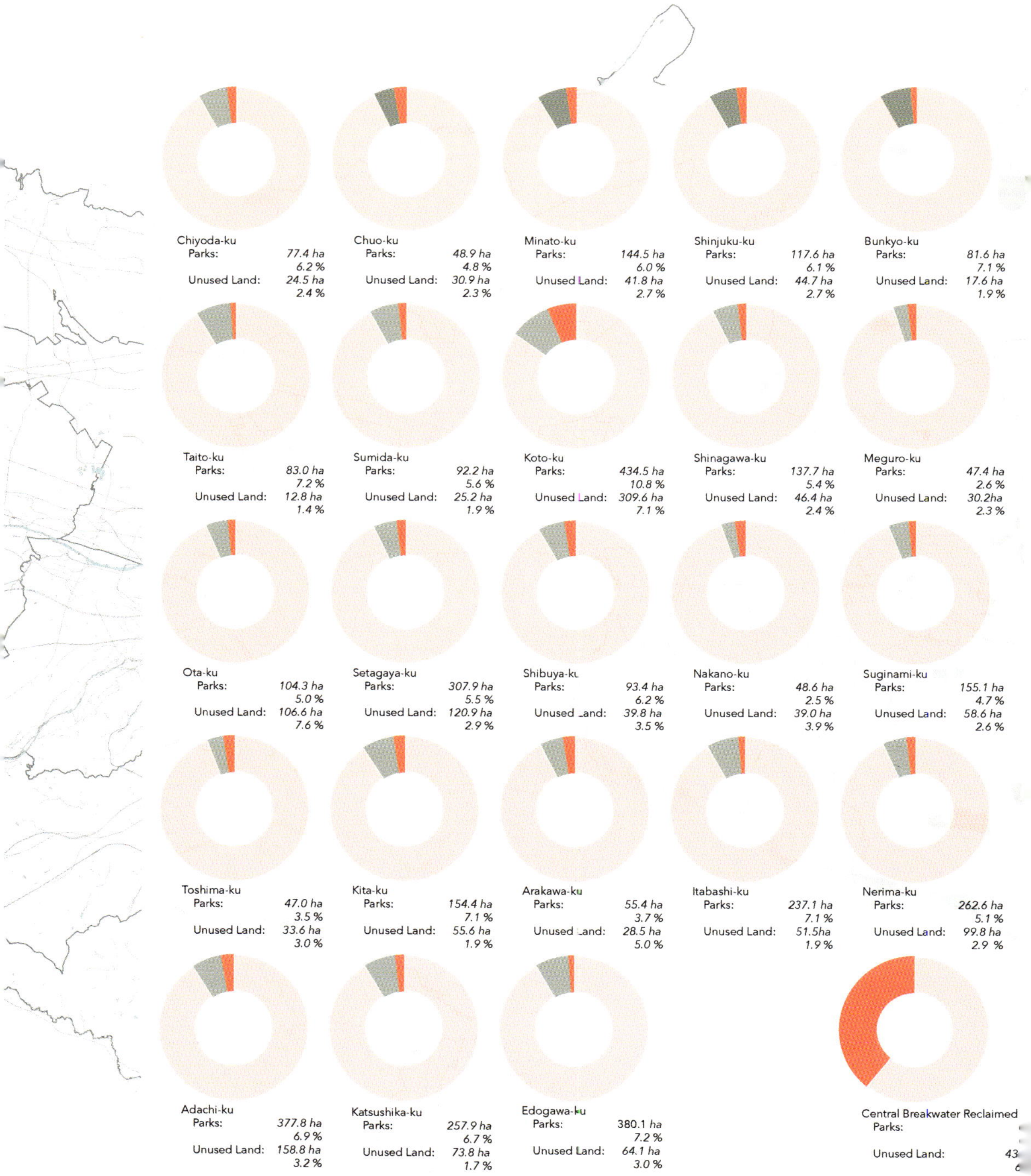

Tokyo's urban park locations, green spaces and unused land data
Map drawing based on GIS data published in 2011
Bureau of the Environment, Tokyo Metropolitan Government

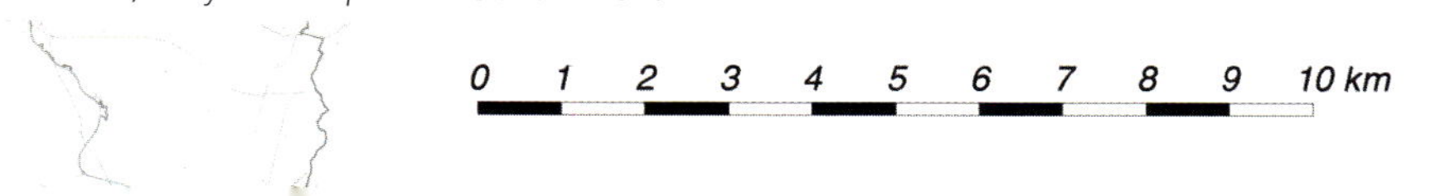

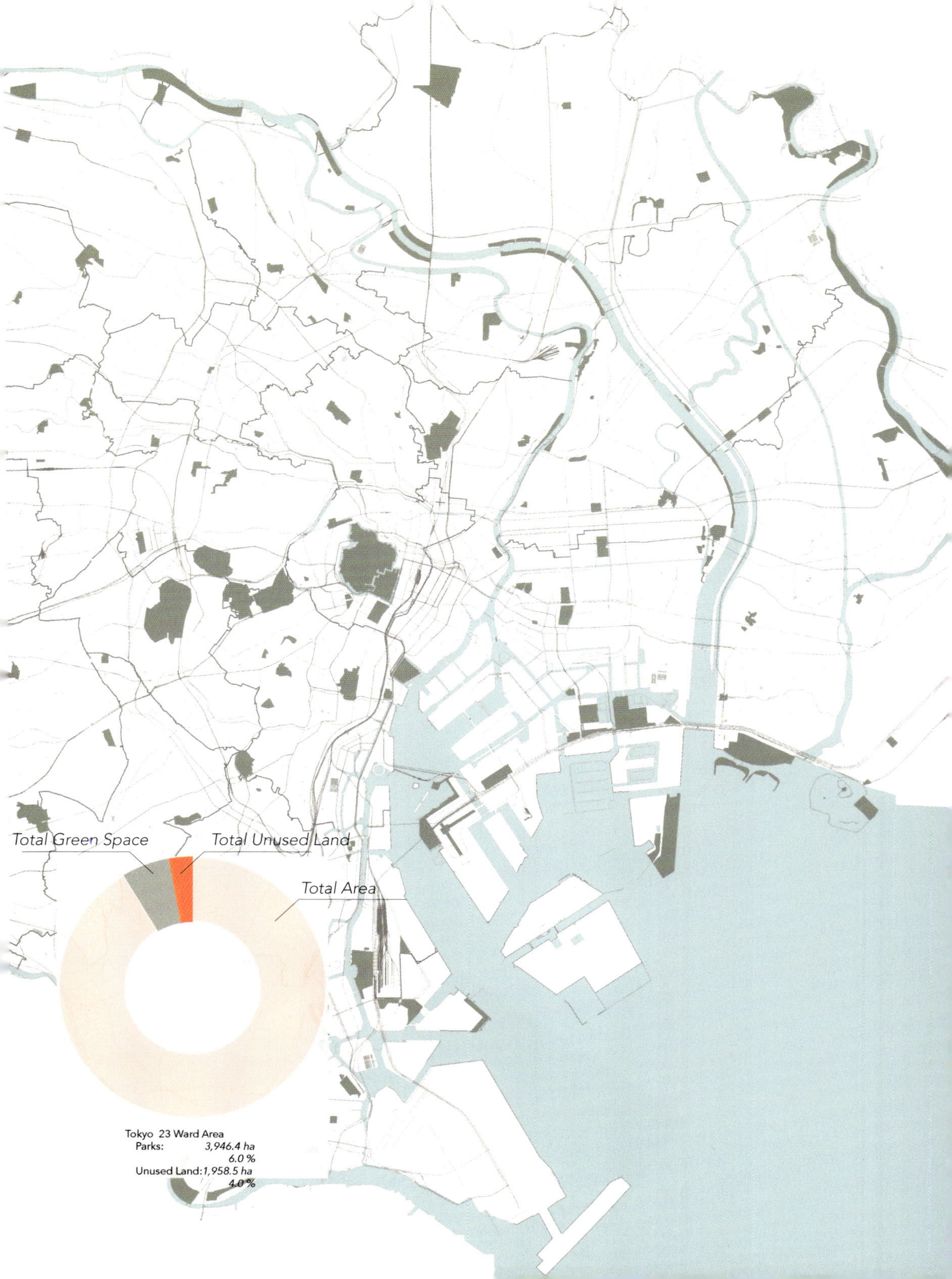
Total Green Space
Total Unused Land
Total Area
Tokyo 23 Ward Area
Parks: 3,946.4 ha
6.0 %
Unused Land: 1,958.5 ha
4.0 %

<20 m²
<50 m²
<100 m²
<500 m²
<1000 m²
30,323.2 m²
Reconstruction Cycle
Road Readjustment
1,796.5 m²
3,319.8 m²
13,864.3 m²
13,864.3 m²
26,849.4 m²
28,683.7 m²
30,721.5 m²
36,933.9 m²
65,041.8 m²
Reclaimed Land
103,549 m²
112,417 m²

Tokyo Urban Void Typologies

Reclaimed land, reconstruction cycles, road readjustment sites mapped in five case study areas between 2009–2013. Toyosu: Reclamation; Shibuya, Taito and Kita wards: Readjustment and reconstruction areas. All sizes in square meters.

The speed of urban- and economic growth before 1995, on one hand, and of the economic stagnation after 1995, on the other hand, determine the factors we see playing out in the production of vacant spaces in Tokyo on broad scales. Yet a few factors have indeed directly influenced the emergence of vacant spaces at a scale that is immediately visible. These leave large tracts of lands undeveloped—although not at a degree seen in many cities in other developed countries—and the politics of urban development have been widely publicized, engaging the wider public in a debate about urban transformation. In most cases, however, the processes are rather slow and an expression of everyday politics.

Each of the different processes informs a distinct set of spatial characteristics. In the course of this exploration, this chapter draws a typology of voids in Tokyo that describes the connection between how these spaces come into being and their spatial appearance. The definition of "unused land" in the land use statistics already points to a particular typology of voids. Summarized here are residential sites prior to construction, sites undergoing zone readjustment, demolition sites, deserted buildings, and reclaimed land. Each of these typologies is routed in distinct socioeconomic and political conditions, which will be discussed in the following sections.

Demographic Trends

Population migration, decentralization, and suburbanization are phenomena that have been attributed to the decline of population and increasing vacancy in inner-city locations. In Tokyo, suburbanization started during the period of rapid urban growth after World War II, which saw a massive influx into the metropolitan region. Those who could afford the higher prices in the city moved to the central areas of Tokyo, while many of those who were leaving rural areas in search of better work and higher education settled in the cheaper outskirts of the city. By the late nineteen-sixties and after years of uncontrolled expansion, the government pushed for the construction of new suburbs—the so-called new towns—in order to accommodate the massive population growth. Simultaneously, private railway companies, which had already started housing developments along newly constructed railway corridors as early as the 1920s, facilitated further suburbanization. Compared to the dense inner-city neighborhoods, these developments not only promised better building standards, but also provided other amenities, such as access to ample green space. The prospect of affordable homeownership in a pleasant environment particularly attracted young families to the suburban developments.

During this time, the population in the central parts of Tokyo continued to grow as well, but when property prices accelerated during the bubble economy, more and more people were forced to leave the city for more affordable property in the suburbs. The population decline in central Tokyo lasted over a decade—until 1996.[5]

As a result, many districts were so severely affected that "craters" were left in the urban landscape.[6] Within Tokyo's twenty-three-ward area, only a few districts were less affected by these demographic changes, some even continued to record a slight population growth. Usually, these were districts at the edge of the municipal boundaries where land prices tend to be lower than in central districts; these include Itabashi and Kita wards, which share a border with Saitama prefecture to the north and have seen steady population growth until recently. Although the population of central Tokyo has been recovering since the late nineteen-nineties, the impact of the massive suburbanization is still evident in the difference between daytime and nighttime populations. Most significant is the difference in the central ward of Chioda, where the daytime population is twenty times higher than the nighttime population.[7] Minato ward, which has seen an increase in new housing developments in recent years, still has five times more people working than living in the area. In Kita ward, on the other hand, the population at night is slightly higher than during the day.

Since the early 2000s, another significant demographic change has informed discussions about the future of many Japanese cities. Similar to other developed nations, Japan's population is shrinking. But in the next couple of decades, the country will face a population decline at an unprecedented scale. According to a report by the National Institute of Population and Social Security Research (IPSS), Japan's population is predicted to decrease by more than 30 percent to 86.74 million people in 2060, compared with 128.06 million in 2010.[8] The shrinkage is amplified by one of the lowest birth rates in the world. Although the fertility rate reached a "sixteen-year high" in 2012 with 1.41 compared to the record low of 1.26 in 2005,[9] this is not enough to balance the impact of the rapidly aging population. Today, the number of senior citizens above sixty-five years already accounts for 23 percent of the population. It is predicted that by 2030, more than one-third of the population will be older then 65 years.[10] By 2060, this figure could increase to 40 percent.

A shrinking population—particularly at this magnitude—will inevitably impact economic and social well-being on many levels. In an editorial titled "Japan's Depopulation Time Bomb," *The Japan Times* outlines how the aging and shrinking society already affects communities, particularly in more rural areas. While maintenance of infrastructural facilities and the provision of social services for the elderly are obvious demands, there is also a necessity for legislative interventions to deal with an increasing number of vacant properties: "Some municipalities have passed by-laws under which they will demolish vacant houses that have become dangerously dilapidated."[11] But as a highly urbanized nation where more than 78 percent of the population lives in cities and metropolitan regions,[12] the impact of the population decline will also be felt in urban areas. In these environments, the massive demographic changes will, as André Sorensen suggests, alter "the meaning of urban space and the urban policy context."[13]

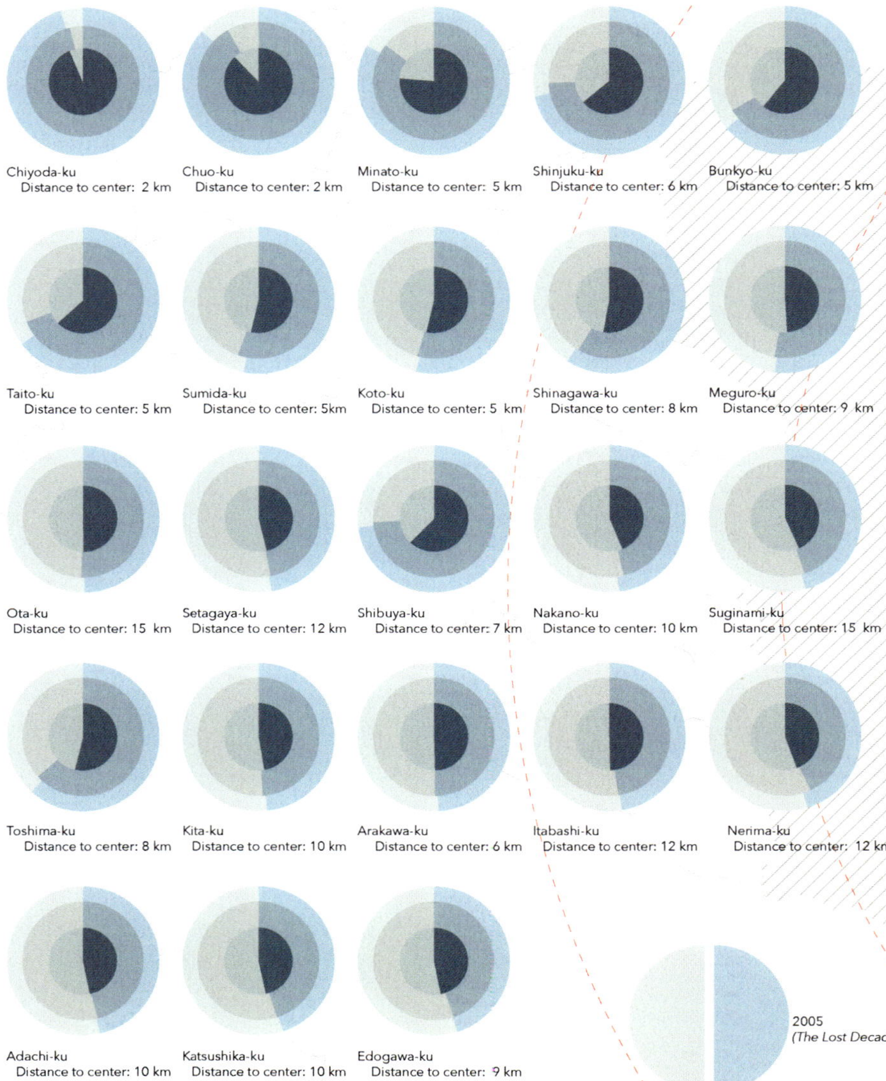

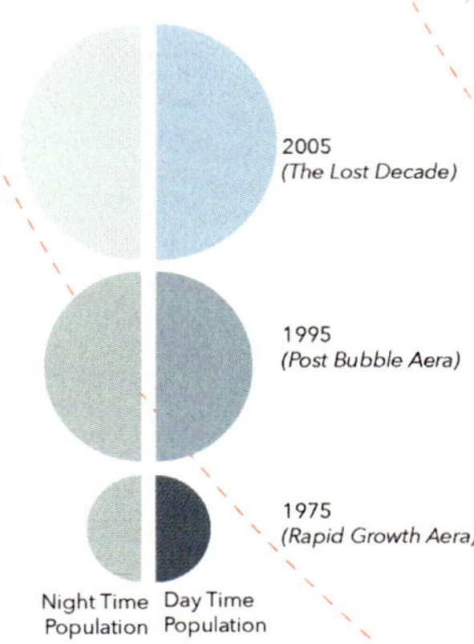

Tokyo Population distribution centers

Night and day time population distribution relative to central Tokyo. Recent shifts occur in central areas such as Shinjuku-ku, Minato-ku due to booming high-rise apartment market.

Tokyo: Population development post 1920

Tokyo Metropolis, Tokyo-to, formed by Tokyo-ku (dark hatch) and Tokyo-shi (light hatch)

Sorensen hypothesizes:

> One primary driver of urban policy will be the imperative to retain and attract population, in attempts to prevent spirals of population and economic decline. If such pressures result in a shift to a prioritisation of urban liveability and quality of life, it would present a major break with the past, as even more than in most developed countries, urban policy in Japan has been focused on economic development and profitability, rather than social infrastructure and quality of place.[14]

So to what extent will these processes affect Tokyo? How do the trends on the national level play out on developments, transformations, and investments in the capital city? And to what extent will Tokyo benefit from the observation that "shrinkage ... opens opportunities."[15]

One of the first research projects that has tried to engage with these questions on the metropolitan level is Fiber City 2050.[16] Through speculative design proposals, this project envisions the future of Tokyo based on a dramatically shrinking and aging society and proposes design strategies—such as land readjustments and activation of vacant spaces through green infrastructure—to counterbalance the negative affects of the population decline. One of the more radical assumptions is that in the near future, parts of the metropolitan highway system will become redundant, and thus available for a transformation into green infrastructure. Overall, these proposals remain highly speculative and focused on future scenarios. Hence, the project reads very much like the big architectural visions of the Metabolism movement, which engaged with contemporary issues through highly futuristic proposals.

The problem with Fiber City 2050 is that it does not indicate how immediate intervention strategies can prepare the ground for its larger ambitions. At the same time, the project applies the national population projections to the capital city. As a result, the project is not grounded enough in the city's current conditions, nor the conditions in the near future. Despite the nation's rapidly declining population, statistical trends for Tokyo suggest that it is not a shrinking city, as such. In effect, "the central areas of the biggest cities are still gaining rather than losing inhabitants ... making for a substantial reurbanisation of the 'craters' caused by earlier suburbanization."[17] In an economically tough climate, it is obvious that large urban agglomerations still have an advantage over smaller rural cities and towns when it comes to economic competitiveness and the provision of social amenities. The centralized nature of the Japanese government, corporate, and higher education sectors made Tokyo the place to which younger generations migrated in search of employment and education opportunities, and this is highly unlikely to change in the future.

Current predictions for Tokyo indicate that the metropolitan region will continue to grow until 2030, and will be the last region in Japan to be affected by the population decline.[18] Although Tokyo's population will be reduced approximately by half over the next ninety years,[19] the city would still have a substantial population of 7.13 million in 2100. Over the past two decades, almost all of the municipalities in the Tokyo metropolis have grown. Only towns in the mountainous regions to the far west, unsuitable for urbanization, have recorded significant losses. By contrast, inner-city areas—in particular those that offer an attractive and livable environment—saw an increase in population. Policy changes initiated by the Koizumi government in the early 2000s, which focused heavily on the strengthening of urban regions, promoted better incentives for private businesses to invest in urban development projects. The easing of restrictions for building heights and floor area ratios has resulted in a condominium construction boom and an increase in inner-city living.

What will most likely cause more significant concerns for Tokyo in the near future is the rapidly aging population. Already today, the impact can be felt, particularly in areas with a large proportion of public housing, the so-called *danchi*, established during the time of rapid urban growth between 1950 and 1980.[20] The Kirigaoka danchi in Kita ward, designed for over 5,000 families, was the biggest public housing project in Tokyo when it was built. Today, the apartments house a record 45 percent elderly population.[21] Considered modern at the time of construction, danchi provided amenities "most Japanese could only dream about,"[22] such as space, light, air, and green areas. But sixty years later, and without any significant refurbishment, these apartments are in decline, and many apartments have already been vacated. In recent years, many blocks have been renovated or reconstructed to provide elevators and barrier-free living for the elderly. A few have been replaced with high-rise condominium towers. But others have simply been torn down, leaving large patches of open land behind.

Reconstruction Cycles

Exemplified in the case of the Kirigaoka danchi is another phenomenon of Japanese urban development. True to the Buddhist philosophy of transience, the real estate market is based on the tradition of rebuilding rather than renovation, keeping the constant cycle of restructuring alive. In Tokyo, this cycle represents the everyday process of urban transformation and is evident everywhere in the city, not only through the large number of construction sites or vacant plots that await construction, but also through the age of the existing building stock. Residential buildings constructed during the postwar period and the era of rapid growth account for only 32 percent of the building stock. Corporate-owned buildings perform only a bit differently with 30 percent of all buildings older than thirty years. Only 6.1 percent of all houses in Tokyo were built before 1960.[23]

The spatially complex and fragmented environment of mostly small, detached residential plots supports constant renewal. This reconstruction is most visible in small properties in residential and traditionally mixed-use neighborhoods. This succession cycle of rebuilding produces the most prevalent type of urban voids: individual, typically small vacant lots. Independent of the neighborhood context, these small lots can remain vacant from just a few weeks to several months, or for many years.

A predominant factor that contributes to the constant rebuilding of residential property is safety concerns with regard to earthquakes or fires. Considering that Tokyo was "flattened" twice during the last century, these events pose a real threat to the city. Despite the low percentage of old buildings outlined above—or probably "Because Japanese houses aren't necessarily expected to last more than 30–40 years"[24]—Tokyo still consists of a large number of inadequately built residences. But the building standards are frequently updated to improve earthquake and fire resistance, especially in areas dominated by cheaply constructed houses of wood, metal sheets, and poorly maintained mortar. Buildings constructed before 1981, when the government introduced major legislative changes to the Building Standards Law, are largely considered unsafe and, according to a survey conducted by the Ministry of Land, Infrastructure, Transport and Tourism, deemed "unfavorable among real estate agents."[25] Demolishing and reconstruction can be seen in any building type, but particularly in traditionally mixed-use housing where small family businesses operate on the ground level, while the upper floors are used for living. When the family's retirement funds become accessible, they replace the building with a new residential dwelling built in accordance with the latest building codes, and often with the extension of another floor.

In other cases, however, where small shops are no longer viable or the owners are simply too old to sustain their business, the vacancy rate increases. This situation can also be observed in a large number of residential properties that rapidly dilapidate, as the mostly elderly owner-occupiers cannot afford the costs to upgrade or renovate their properties. When they move to nursery homes, and after their deaths, many of these properties fall vacant, because there is little incentive for the inheritors to renovate or redevelop the homes before the property is sold.[26] Presently, the Japanese taxation system still heavily supports the construction of new homes, making the acquisition of existing buildings less attractive for potential buyers. In addition, property taxes on vacant land is higher than on land with a built structure, therefore many buildings are not immediately torn down even if they already uninhabitable.

Where building standards and amenities no longer meet the social demands, the cycle of rebuilding is disrupted. In formerly densely built areas, increasingly larger patches of vacant land now appear leaving a pattern of openness. In contrast to the Fiber City 2050 proposal, this situation only occurs in inner-city neighborhoods—mainly "in older industrial inner areas," as Sorensen observes.[27] The hardest hit communities in the metropolitan region are located in the outer suburban areas and neighborhoods constructed during the time of rapid urban growth.

Acknowledging the impact vacancies have on declining neighborhood quality and economic viability, the government in recent years has started to "promote reform, renovation, and other efforts to improve real estate value by improving and revitalizing both the real estate investment market and the real estate distribution market."[28] Sorensen suggests a more comprehensive alternative. Calling the decline of highly attractive neighborhoods with good infrastructure a "waste," he proposes that in addition to small-scale renovation and replacement, some vacant properties should be "used to create new public spaces, some to provide more spacious new housing for in-migrants and others to combine some tiny plots into larger ones."[29] Landscape characteristics, such as an increase in greenery, are strongly tied to attractiveness, and as environmental concerns become increasingly important drivers in sustaining neighborhoods and preventing decline, vacant space provides the opportunity to increase "breathing" space, neighborhood popularity, and property value.

In this light, private investment in the real estate market plays an increasingly important role in shaping Japanese cities. One of the most prolific figures in the building industry is Minoru Mori, whose "Vertical Garden City"[30] vision is certainly among the most radical developer-driven proposals for Tokyo. Reconstruction projects of this nature are commonly based on readjustments of land to combine smaller properties into larger residential or mixed-use complexes. Due to the complex ownership structure, the involved land acquisition and compensation process is not only expensive, but also often incredibly time consuming, causing an increasing number of smaller vacant plots before the construction can eventually commence.

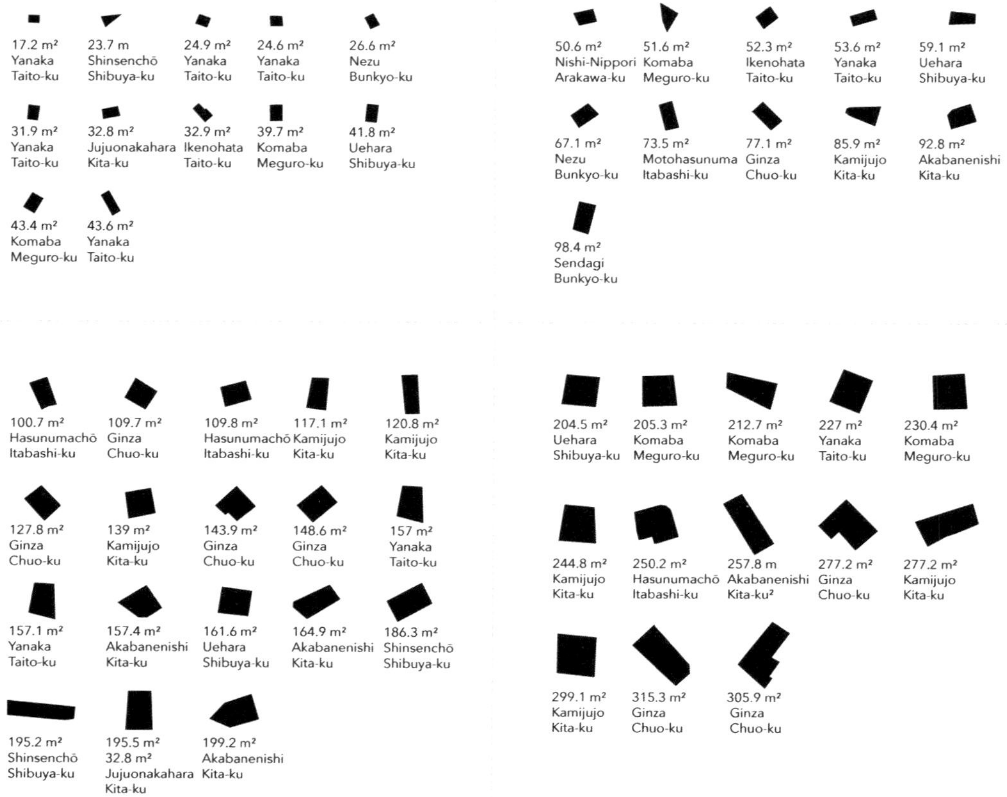

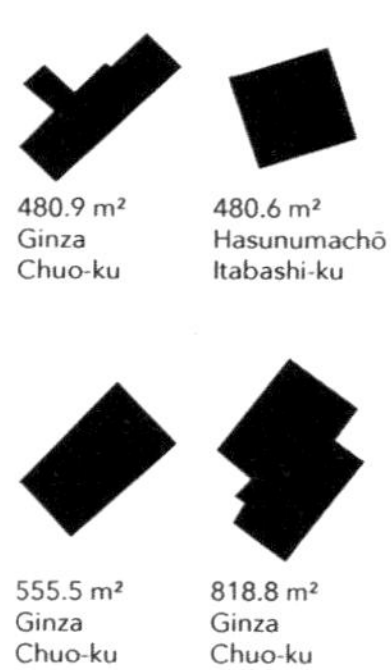

Tokyo's Urban Void Typologies
Urban reconstruction and renewal processes produce fragmented and mostly small scale voids. Voids recorded in five areas between 2009–2013.

Urban renewal processes + vending machine economy
Shopping Arcade, Kita-ku, 2012

Wasteland Transformations

Tokyo's foreshore area is under constant redevelopment and presents large tracts of open land at a scale that is otherwise unseen in the city. Constructed to meet the demands of a rapidly growing city, the artificial islands provided land for new housing, as well as commercial and industrial use. However, vast areas of this reclaimed landscape are still vacant or undeveloped. How do these spaces come into being? What strategies exist to deal with the land? And why can a city that is pressured for space afford this amount of vacant space? While the progressive development of the bay area occurred in different periods, land reclamation was based on the common principle of growth. The vacant spaces we see today, however, are a result of very different circumstances and highlight three trajectories for vacancy. First, political objectives in urban development profoundly influenced the construction of large-scale housing and commercial projects in the Tokyo Bay area. In these districts, vacant spaces are synonyms for exaggerated dreams and failed aspirations. Second, the effects of deindustrialization became most visible in this part of the city as heavy industry and production predominantly settled in the Tokyo Port area. Cleared of all industrial traces, these sites now present a very different landscape than the rest of the city, with vast open skies and jungles of remnant vegetation. The third trajectory is connected to the outlook on Tokyo's waste management. Tokyo Bay continues to be used as a dumping and treatment area for the massive amount of waste produced in the city. Void spaces here are still in the making.

Urban and Industrial Growth

Land reclamation has a long history in Tokyo, dating back to the Edo period (1603–1867) when large areas of land were created in districts that today make up parts of the inner-city wards of Chuo, Minato, and Koto. A major increase in land acquisition can be seen in the years following World War II, when large islands emerged to provide land for Tokyo's rapid industrial and commercial growth. With increasing industrial productivity in the nineteen-sixties and nineteen-seventies, this was also the time of mass consumption, which resulted in the massive production of waste "much of which was dumped in the bay."[31] Another major trigger of expansion occurred during the nineteen-eighties, driven by the general development and economic growth in Japan. The progress of the Japanese bubble economy and massive investment in the real estate sector further spurred the reclamation of artificial islands. During this time, as Seguchi writes, land reclamation was also part of a larger political and corporate agenda to "increase their power to exploit the waterfront."[32] Large marine projects, which could be linked to central city areas and developed with the support of proactive metropolitan governments, held the promise of substantial development profits."[33] Yet, while in previous eras the amount of reclaimed land seemed to be in balance with the demand at the respective time, the inflated market during the nineteen-eighties led to a massive oversupply of commercial and residential land. Many projects

Wasteland Transformations, Odaiba, Chuo-ku, 2009

subsequently stagnated or never commenced in the first place. Due to the economic recession that followed the bust of the bubble, strategies for redeveloping these sites never really picked up again leaving most of the bay area in a state that Julian Worrall and Erez Golani Solomon poignantly describe as "tabula rasa for the projection of planners' fantasies, a vacant lot for industrial expansion, and a dumping ground for Tokyo's garbage."[34]

Failed political ideologies played out most notably in the redevelopment efforts of the Tokyo Waterfront Subcenter. Covering an area of 448 hectares, the Waterfront Subcenter comprises two artificial islands, more commonly known as Odaiba and Ariake. Reclaimed between 1946 and 1975, these prominent districts today feature major shopping, entertainment, as well as international convention and exhibition facilities. For the most part, however, this development represents only a fraction of the original master plan.

Discussions around a comprehensive redevelopment of landfill sites had already begun in the nineteen-sixties with Kenzo Tange's proposal for a futuristic expansion of the city into the bay. Sustained efforts, however, only took off when the Tokyo Metropolitan Government, under the leadership of governor Shuichi Suzuki, started to redesign this area into a new district for recreational and commercial use. Close to the city center, the Waterfront City was planned as a high-tech living showcase for 6,300 inhabitants and a working population of 106,000.[35] The central concept was based on the idea of technology, innovation, and international exchange. Each of the four districts that encompass this project was designed to accommodate the assigned activities embedded in a distinct urban character. Odaiba largely evolved around recreational facilities, while the adjacent Aomi district to the south provided space for commercial enterprises, especially in the information and media sector. The second island was divided into two districts: one with a mostly residential focus (Ariake-North), and one that would house convention and exhibition facilities (Ariake-South).

As inner-city districts faced increasing environmental problems and bad living quality as a result of the rapid urban growth—including high density, lack of space, bad air quality, and massive traffic congestions—the first Waterfront Subcenter was envisioned as a better place and alternative to the rest of the city. Consequently, the first master plan layout included medium-rise density interspersed with ample open space for recreational use and access to the waterfront, and possessed none of the intricacy and small-grain urban fabric seen in central Tokyo. With the bubble economy in full swing, authorities further amended the original plans and started to respond to the economic climate with its appreciation for grandeur and exaggeration. Signature corporate architecture—for example, the futuristic Fuji Television building or the Tokyo Big Sight convention and exhibition center—alongside open space in the style of the grand avenues, promenades, and skywalks illustrate today only too well the style and spirit of the time.

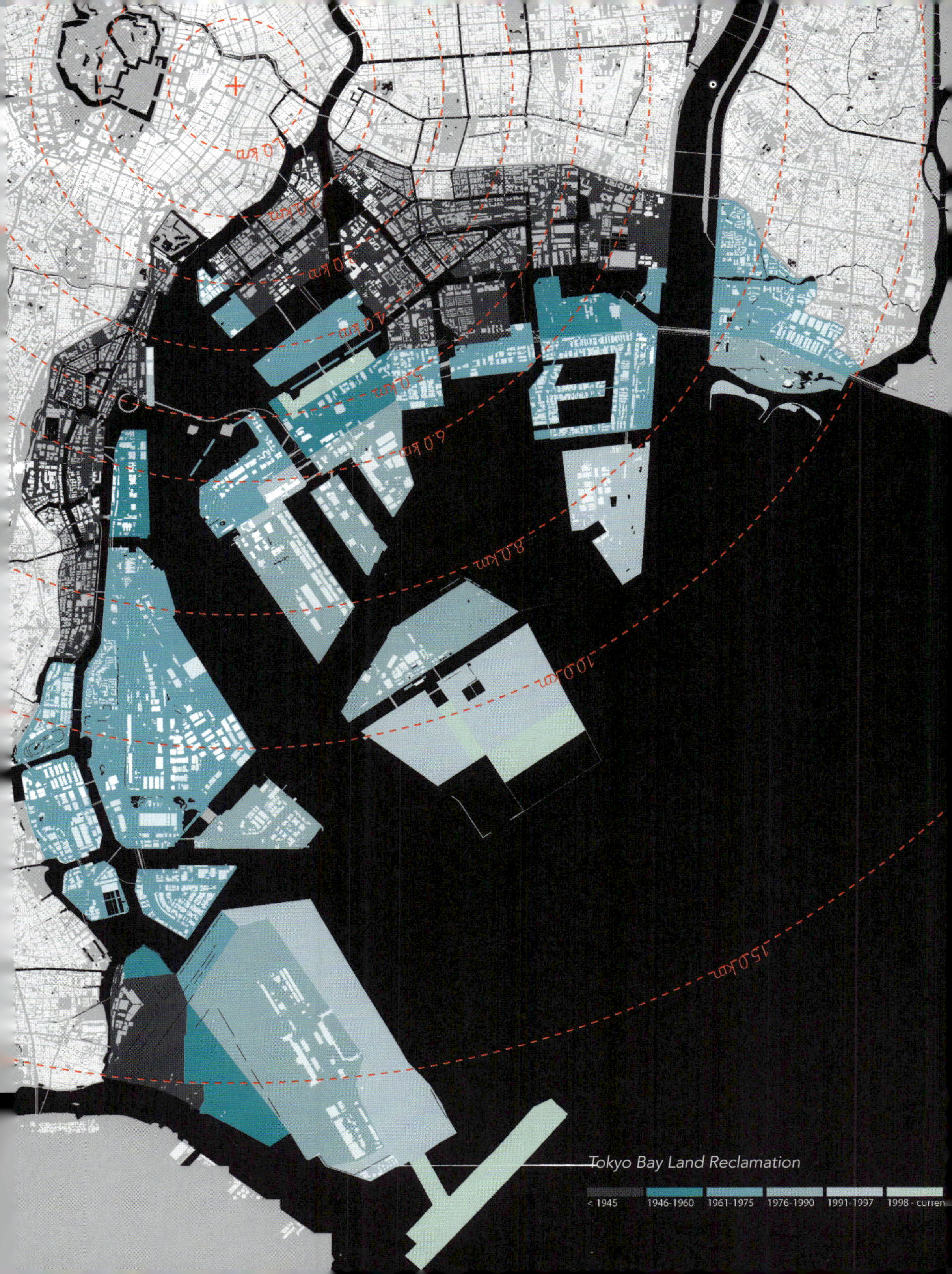

4.0 km
5.0 km
6.0 km
8.0 km
10.0 km
15.0 km
Tokyo Bay Land Reclamation
< 1945
1946-1960
1961-1975
1976-1990
1991-1997
1998 - curren

Yet, by the time these buildings were completed, the Japanese economy was already in rapid decline. By the beginning of nineteen-nineties, many newly constructed commercial buildings in Tokyo already faced a low occupancy rate forcing a halt in countless development projects. In addition, an increasingly critical public began to question the purpose of these big investments in times of economic uncertainty. With little support remaining, the governor used the planned International City Exposition "Urban Frontier" as an argument to move the development ahead. Seguchi notes that the Expo, scheduled for 1996 and equally unpopular with the public, was only a political initiative "intended to promote the project and to launch its convention and exhibition facilities."[36] But due to increasing political and economic pressure, the Expo was first postponed, then scaled down, and finally cancelled in 1995. Today, it is a synonym for the decline of the Waterfront City Subcenter and highlights the failure of the very political aspirations that initiated the project in the first place.

In the past few years, the Japanese economy has shown the first, slow signs of recovery. At the same time, Tokyo eventually won its bid to host the Summer Olympics in 2020, after a previously unsuccessful application for the games in 2016. In both proposals, the bay area plays a major role, not only as sporting venue during the games but also as part of the Olympic Legacy. While these factors contribute to a regained economic confidence that encourages new construction projects, the longevity of this trend remains uncertain. The fundamental question is whether Japan's economic climate is strong enough for a sustained urban development that continues after the hype of the Olympic games has faded. Today, it still remains unclear when the Waterfront City Subcenter will ultimately be completed and how the original plans will alter due to the Olympic legacy. According to the Tokyo Municipal Government's (TMG) predictions, a living population of 47,000 and a working population of 90,000 are estimated for the Waterfront City Subcenter by 2016.[37] This reflects an increase of more than 600 percent in residential numbers and 300 percent in the working population compared to 2007. Despite a condominium tower boom that has shaped some recent developments in the area, a large number of vacant plots remain, making it hard to imagine that the projected target will be achieved in time. Overstated political agendas and unrealistic projections may continue to cause problems for large-scale redevelopments.

Postindustrial Landscape

While the Waterfront City Subcenter is an exceptional case study on many levels, most of the reclaimed land in the bay area has undergone a very different—and less publicized—transformation process. Developed around industrial production, much of the reclaimed land was occupied by heavy industry, such as steel production, coal shipment, gas production, and container shipment. The vacant land we see here today is a direct result of deindustrialization processes as companies relocated their production to outer suburbs or to other prefectures in the Kanto region, where land prices are significantly lower and better connected to infrastructural facilities.

While many places in the US and Europe faced a "mass exodus from older urban, industrialized areas," which dramatically changed the "physical appearance of cities,"[38] deindustrialization processes in Tokyo never disrupted the urban fabric to the same extent. This does not mean that manufacturing or industrial productivity does not occur in inner-city districts. In fact, many neighborhoods—particularly in the eastern part of the city—are developed around industrial businesses. The traditional link between commercial, industrial, and residential use, however, established a manufacturing industry on a very small scale. Until today, many family-owned businesses focus on the production of highly specialized products and manufacturing processes, and continue to operate out of small workshop spaces. Dominated by small and medium-size businesses, large parts of Tokyo resemble what Sorensen calls a "high degree of intermixture of seemingly incompatible land uses."[39] Even larger facilities, like waste incineration plants, can be found in residential neighborhoods. However, industries that depended on extensive land and good waterfront access to ship their products through the Port of Tokyo were usually located along the waterfront of the rivers and in Tokyo Bay. Consequently, large-scale deindustrialization today concentrates on reclaimed land outside of the city center.

Despite their central location, these sites were poorly connected to the rest of the city and were for a long time not quite considered a part of the city. Only the construction of roads and public transport infrastructure, commencing with the closure of heavy industry, brought the islands closer to the heart of the city. Toyosu, an artificial island located approximately five kilometers from the city center is an example of Tokyo's postindustrial landscape. Completed in 1954, the site consists of two areas. The area to the north was occupied by a shipbuilding factory. After the factory shut down, Mistui Fudosan purchased the site and began redeveloping the area into a new residential and commercial district. After a slow start in the nineteen-nineties, the development now houses a major shopping and entertainment facility, as well as several high-rise condominium and office towers. While vacant sites in this area have decreased significantly with construction activity, the demand for high-rise living in Toyosu has stalled after the 2011 earthquake caused significant damage and liquefaction in Tokyo Bay.[40]

In contrast to the developments around the Toyosu station in the north, the island to the southwest is still a barren landscape. This area was occupied by Tokyo Gas, which operated their business here between 1956 and 1994, when the company eventually moved its production to the outer suburbs. As Paul Waley notes, heritage conservation does not sit high on Tokyo's planning and design agenda.[41] Thus, it is not surprising that in preparation for future developments in Toyosu, most industrial traces were cleared.

Postindustrial Landscape, Toyosu, Chuo-ku, 2012

While the northern part maintains a few industrial features and artifacts, all structures, buildings, offices, gas towers, and rail tracks that occupied the southern land were cleared. Even the docks where coal ships previously landed were rebuilt to provide a smoother shoreline. The loss of Tokyo's heavy industry was immediately followed by the burst of the economic bubble, and by the time Tokyo Gas relocated its business the economy was already in rapid decline leaving the site vacant for almost twenty years. In 2011, the TMG finally decided to purchase the site to relocate the Tokyo Wholesale and Fish market, but financial resources are scarce and the project is highly unpopular with the public. Among other issues, concerns over soil contamination challenge and further postpone any anticipated development.

Wastelands in Production

Land reclamation in Tokyo Bay has always been synonymous with the consumerist society and its massive production of waste. Despite significant efforts to reduce the overall amount of waste, Tokyo will continue to depend on further landfill sites in the future; but space in Tokyo Bay is running out. While the TMG is committed to further expansion of landfill projects in the bay as a means to handle the city's massive garbage production, it acknowledges the increasing difficulty in locating suitable areas. Only two reclamation sites are currently in operation: the Outer Central Breakwater landfill site and New Sea Surface Disposal Site. The latter, which is a 480-hectare site and can store 120 cubic meters of waste, is considered to be the last land reclamation project in Tokyo Bay.

It will be a while before the New Sea Surface Disposal Site reaches its capacity, but in recent years the government has started intensive campaigns to further manage the volume of waste. Recycling has already had a major impact on the reduction. Almost 99 percent of construction materials, such as concrete and asphalt, are currently recycled. The amount of household waste has been significantly reduced and only accounts for a fraction of the overall material disposed in landfill sites. The major challenge for the city continues to be the handling of its industrial waste.

As part of the "3R" strategy (reduce, reuse, and recycle), which promotes more resourceful management of material, the government initiated in 2002 the Super Eco-Town; the project includes new facilities to efficiently handle and dispose of industrial waste through advanced recycling technologies. According to the TMG, this project aims "to solve waste problems, foster environmental industry, and transform the society into one based on recycling."[42] In several facilities around Tokyo Bay, the waste is treated in specialized procedures.

Soil decontamination at future site of Tokyo Wholesale and Fish Market
Toyosu, Chuo-ku, 2012

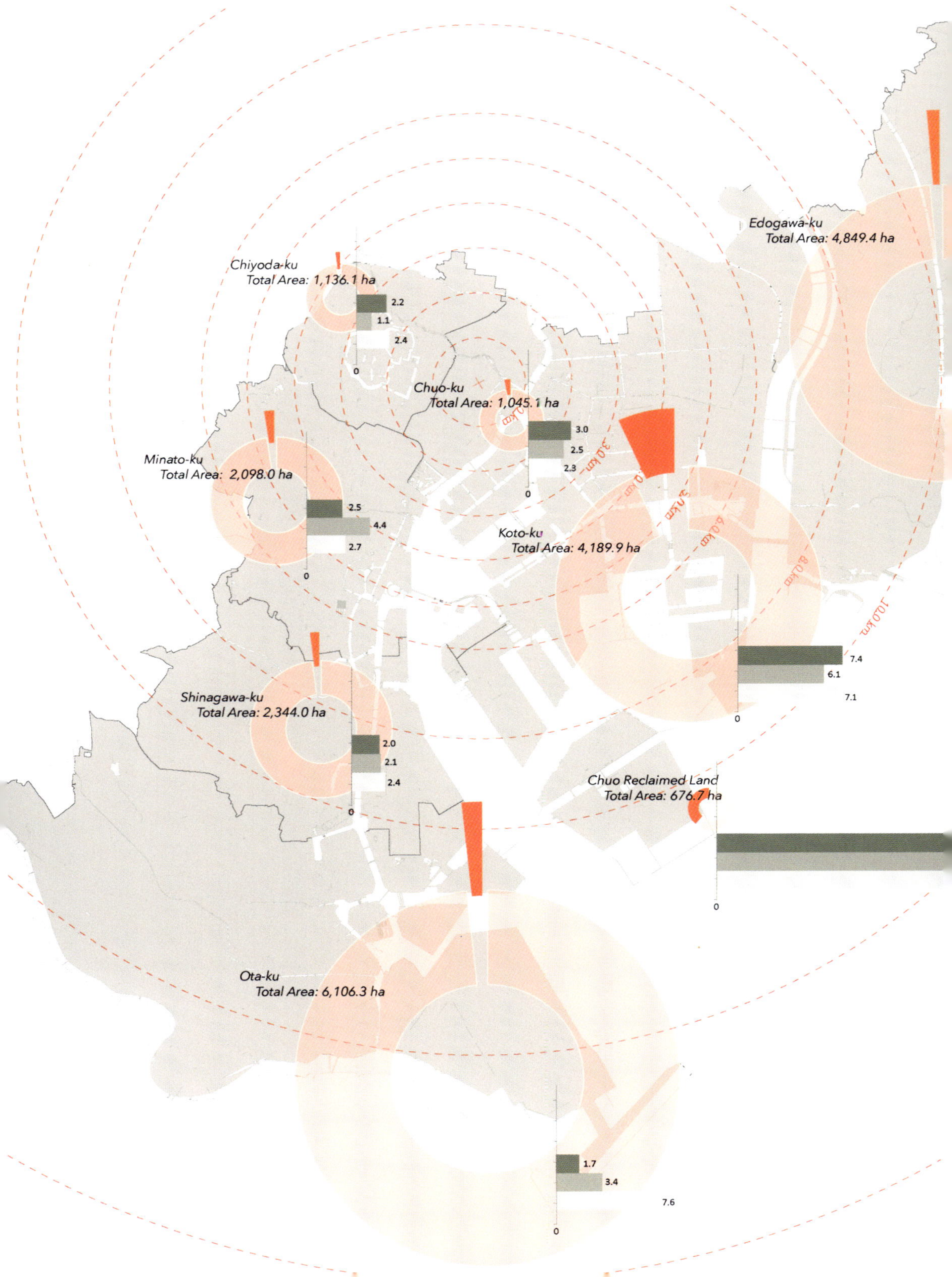

Edogawa-ku
Total Area: 4,849.4 ha
Chiyoda-ku
Total Area: 1,136.1 ha
2.2
1.1
2.4
0
Chuo-ku
Total Area: 1,045.1 ha
3.0
2.5
2.3
0
Minato-ku
Total Area: 2,098.0 ha
2.5
4.4
2.7
0
Koto-ku
Total Area: 4,189.9 ha
3.0 km
6.0 km
8.0 km
10.0 km
7.4
6.1
7.1
0
Shinagawa-ku
Total Area: 2,344.0 ha
2.0
2.1
2.4
0
Chuo Reclaimed Land
Total Area: 676.7 ha
0
Ota-ku
Total Area: 6,106.3 ha
1.7
3.4
7.6
0

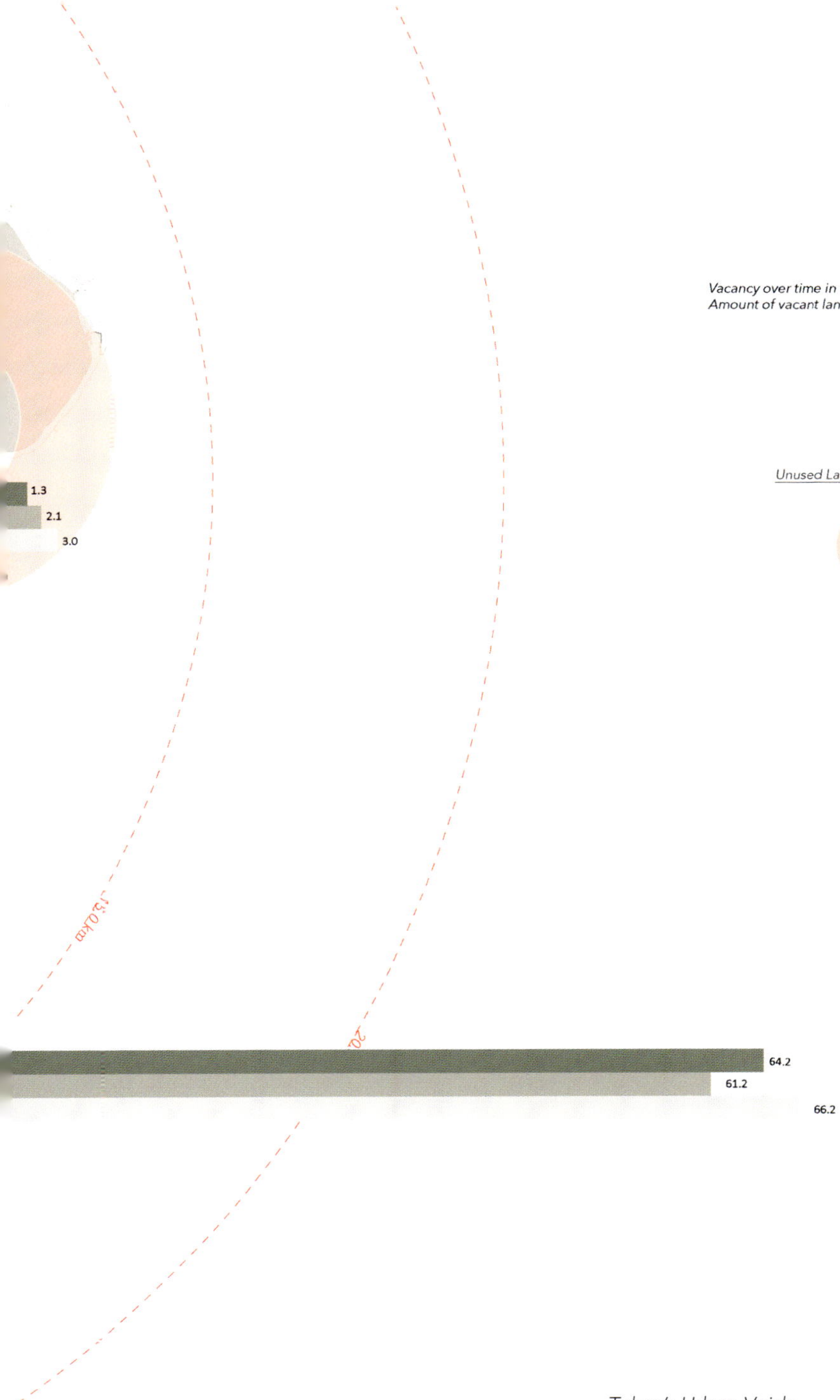

Vacancy over time in wards built on substantial land reclamation.
Amount of vacant land in percentage by year

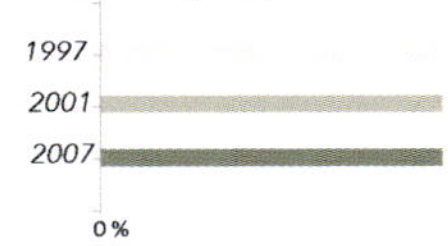

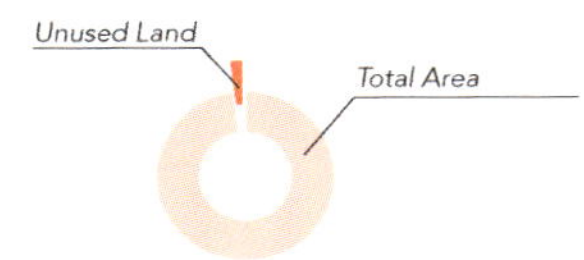

Tokyo's Urban Voids
Vacant/unused land relative to overall area of ward.
Tokyo Metropolitan Statistics, GIS Data, 1997–2007

One such facility is located on the Chuo Breakwater site, which houses a PCB treatment plant and the Tokyo Waterfront Recycle Power Company, an incineration facility that treats plastics and demolition debris from construction sites, as well as infectious medical waste. Other ventures that follow the 3R strategy include the afforestation project Umi no Mori (discussed in Chapter One). Most of these facilities engage in programs to raise public awareness of the environmental issues associated with waste production, handling, and recycling. While Umi no Mori invites elementary schools to participate in planting activities, other facilities offer educational programs and provide guided tours for the public.

With these initiatives, the latest reclamation sites can hardly be classified as postindustrial sites. Vacancy here does not occur due to deindustrialization, as in Toyosu, or as a consequence of stagnant economic development. Instead, there is a shift from manufacturing industries to other types of industrial businesses. The mechanisms that inform the development and transition of this area are again based on the principle of growth. This is further reflected in the future land use plan for the New Sea Surface Disposal Site, which clearly demonstrates the new ambitions. As a further extension of the Umi no Mori project and Ando's greenbelt proposal to boost better wind passages from the sea to the central Tokyo, the western disposal site will be redeveloped into an extensive green space. The area to the east will house facilities for a new container port, despite the fact that the city government acknowledges its challenging position in the increasingly competitive market. Tokyo Port has already lost its position as a leading East Asian port to cities with better geographic locations, such as Busan (Korea) and Shanghai (China). Moreover, under the current economic conditions, the extension of a container port seems less convincing. In the long run, we may continue to see large areas of vacant land in Tokyo's Bay.

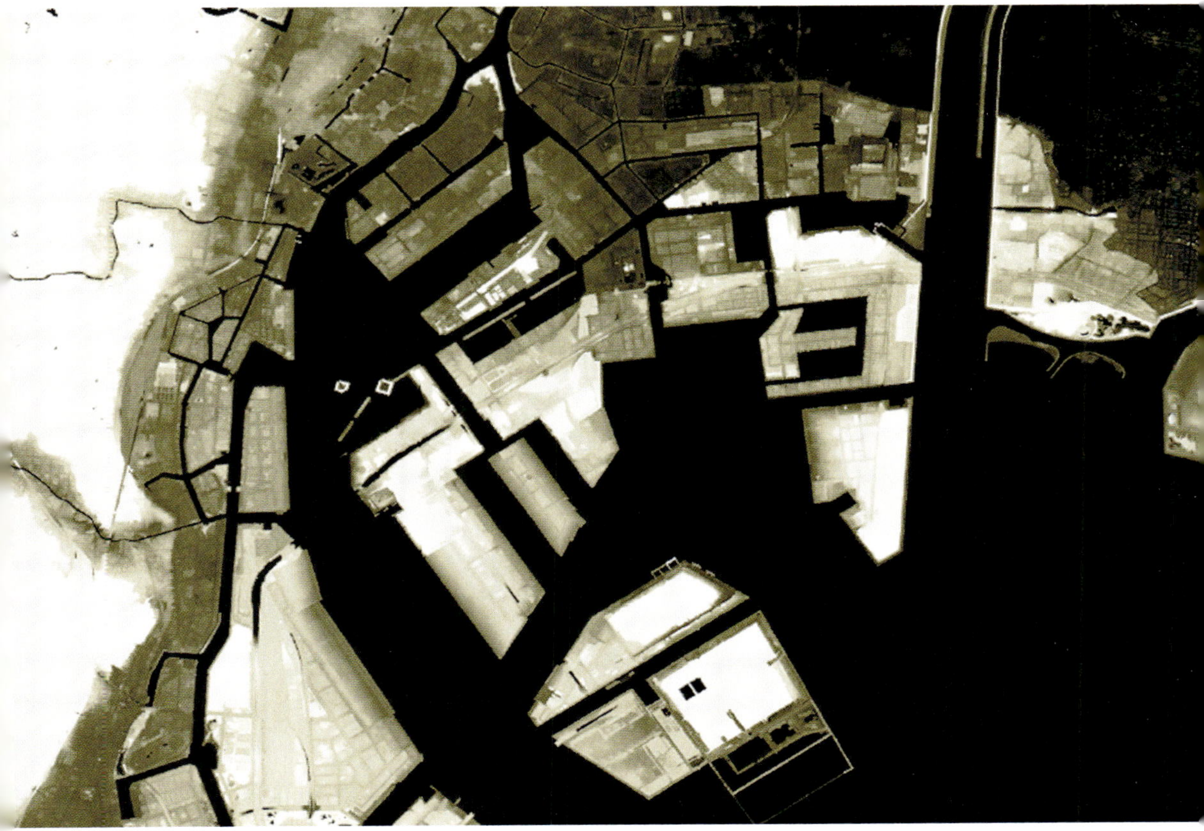

Tokyo Bay Land Reclamation Sites
Topography generated through land reclamation in Tokyo Bay.
Lighter areas are showing higher ground, darker areas low land.
GIS data + Kashmir3D, reproduced with permission of Hajime Ishikawa.

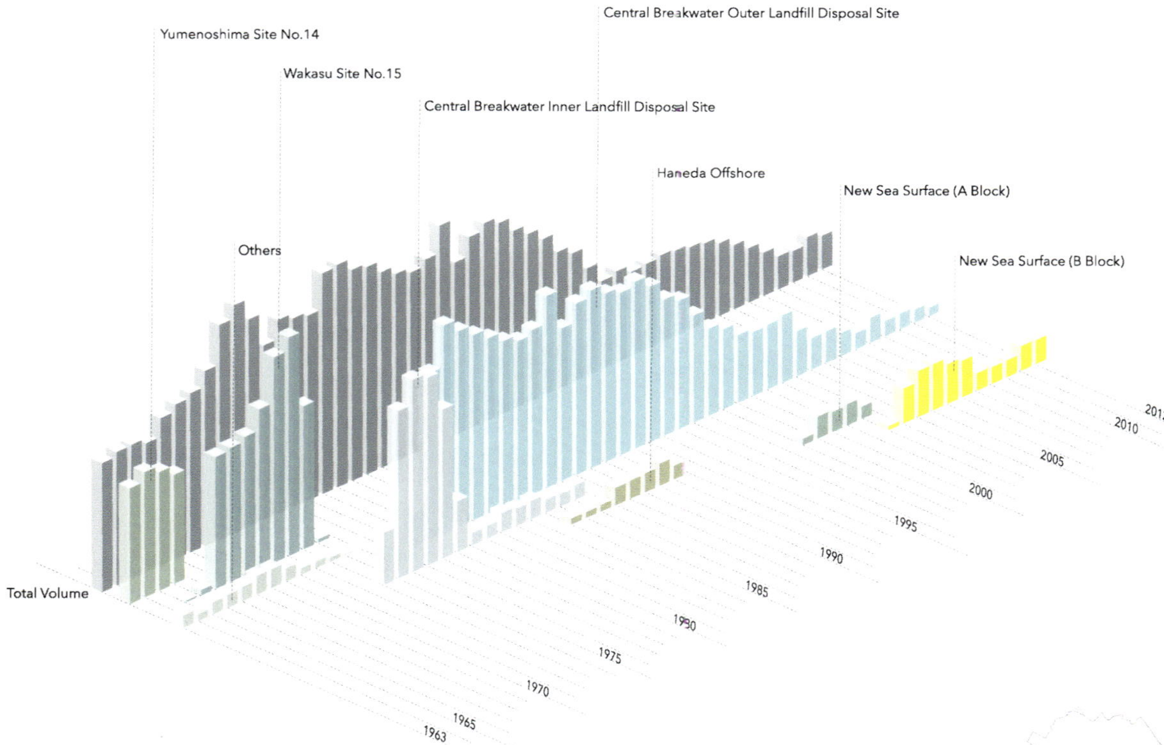

year of operation	Others	Yumenoshima Site No.14	Wakasu Site No.15	Central Breakwater Inner Landfill Disposal Site	Central Breakwater Outer Landfill Disposal Site	Haneda Offshore	New Sea Surface (A Block)	New Sea Surface (B Block)
01	1963 20	1963 181	1965 3	1973 81	1977 53	1984 10	1998 11	2002 7
02	1964 12	1964 196	1966 9	1974 260	1978 260	1985 10	1999 35	2003 56
03	1965 20	1965 186	1967 207	1975 298	1979 323	1986 11	2000 32	2004 73
04	1966 21	1966 171	1968 211	1976 291	1980 304	1987 28	2001 34	2005 73
05	1967 23		1969 218	1977 232	1981 288	1988 29	2002 20	2006 63
06	1968 30		1970 251	1978 80	1982 273	1989 30		2007 58
07	1969 30		1971 321	1979 20	1983 258	1990 35		2008 28
08	1970 21		1972 341	1980 21	1984 248	1991 22		2009 27
09	1971 11		1973 225	1981 31	1985 255			2010 27
10	1972 11		1974 6	1982 28	1986 297			2011 39
11	1973 7			1983 30	1987 237			2012 38
12	1974 2			1984 22	1988 265			
13	1975 1			1985 20	1989 275			
14				1986 24	1990 260			
15					1991 251			
16					1992 258			
17					1993 240			
18					1994 210			
19					1995 198			
20					1996 165			
21					1997 135			
22					1998 124			
23					1999 105			
24					2000 99			
25					2001 100			
26					2002 104			
26					2003 70			
27					2004 49			
28					2005 49			
29					2006 36			
30					2007 26			
31					2008 39			
32					2009 24			
33					2010 25			
34					2011 21			
35					2012 14			

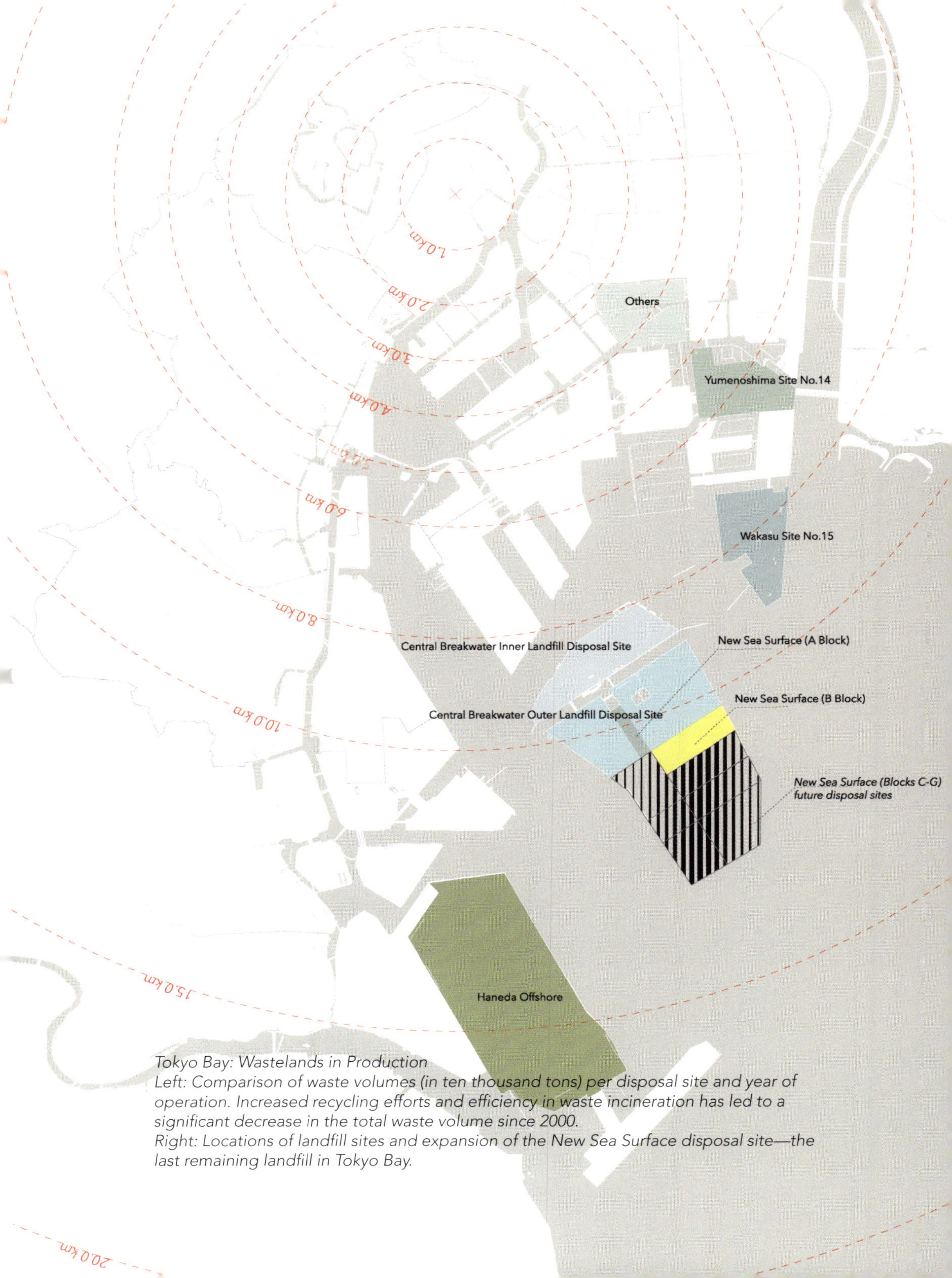

Tokyo Bay: Wastelands in Production
Left: Comparison of waste volumes (in ten thousand tons) per disposal site and year of operation. Increased recycling efforts and efficiency in waste incineration has led to a significant decrease in the total waste volume since 2000.
Right: Locations of landfill sites and expansion of the New Sea Surface disposal site—the last remaining landfill in Tokyo Bay.

Road readjustment for the new auxiliary road in Kitazawa, Setagaya-ku and Uehara, Shibuya-ku, 2009–ongoing. The fence, left in the image, protects cleared plots along the narrow street.

Road Readjustments

A large number of void spaces are the product of planning strategies and improvements to Tokyo's urban infrastructure. Most notable are the effects of road-widening projects, which lead to awkward spatial configurations and produce voids as fragmented strips of land along one or both sides of the street. In practice, readjustment plans are overlaid on existing building infrastructure, which requires the government to compensate affected owners. As buildings are demolished, the vacant spaces are cleared, covered in asphalt, and enclosed with either high fences or lower railings.

In most cases, these projects occur in densely built neighborhoods with a high proportion of wooden housing, interspersed with narrow streets often less than two meters wide. With the building stock being both highly flammable and easy collapsible, and with difficult emergency access through the narrow streets, these are high-risk areas during earthquakes and fires. Since the devastation of the 1923 Great Kanto Earthquake, the importance of road infrastructure has been recognized as a disaster mitigation strategy—both as a means of providing evacuation routes and preventing the spread of fires.

An indirect cause of voids in these communities is the specific setback rules. In the process of road readjustments, the setback rules specify a certain percentage or size of area to be acquired for road widening. According to central legislation, a road in Japan should be at least four meters wide. Depending on the existing street width, the setbacks in densely built neighborhoods often claim a significant proportion of the already small plot size. In some cases, the plot is reduced so significantly that conventional construction becomes ineffective and the plot therefore remains vacant. In contrast to the larger road development projects, where the successive acquisition of land initially produces single gaps and later larger strips of voids, the setback rules result in mainly small, single vacant plots.

The city government has identified several exceptionally vulnerable neighborhoods as priority areas where improvements to the transport infrastructure should "bolster earthquake—and disaster—resistance."[43] The area around Jujo station in Kita ward has been identified a one of the priority areas for urban regeneration, and involves the redevelopment of a 2.6-kilometer road transect between Akabane station and Kita Naka Jujo. The project includes the expansion of the traffic lanes to eleven meters and the provision of previously absent sidewalks of 4.5 meters on each side of the road. Here, the road widening is only one aspect of a comprehensive urban planning strategy. It also includes other infrastructural redevelopments to strengthen the neighborhood's disaster resilience, including large-scale emergency facilities. In these so-called integrated developments that form part of the larger urban renewal strategy, the government strategically seeks to increase the influence of the private sector.

Tokyo's Urban Void Typologies
Documented road readjustment voids in five case study areas 2009–2013

Auxiliary Road 26 in Kitazawa, Setagaya-ku and Uehara, Shibuya-ku
Process of land acquisition and clearance as of 2012.

Kita-ku, 2010

Shibuya-ku, 2011

Shibuya-ku, 2010

Shibuya-ku, 2012

Shibuya-ku, 2010

Shibuya-ku, 2010

Kita-ku, 2011

Kita-ku, 2011

Shibuya-ku, 2010

Kita-ku, 2012

Shibuya-ku, 2010

Shibuya-ku, 2012

Road Readjustment Structures

The reconstruction of housing along the road that replaces the predominantly wooden homes with reinforced concrete buildings is only one aspect of how private developers are involved in these projects. Other investments focus on the commercialization of the outskirts, by encouraging the establishment of private businesses or even entire shopping malls.

As a city built on the principles of efficiency, Tokyo's urban planning and design strategies are concerned with rather pragmatic considerations. While Tokyo already has one of the most advanced train network infrastructures in the world, road traffic continues to raise concerns. Increasing traffic volume and lack of pedestrian sidewalks continue to disrupt the efficiency and cause road safety issues. In 1999, the average travel speed during rush hour in the Tokyo 23-ward area was only 17.5 kilometers per hour. In 2005, the situation had improved only slightly to 20.4 kilometers per hour,[44] while the road traffic census of 2010 states an average speed of only 16.8 kilometers per hour.[45] In light of this poor performance and the continuous pressure of congestion, the city is committed to improving the traffic flow by expanding the road network and reducing the disruption at train level crossings. More efficiency is anticipated by creating new arterial roads. In many neighborhoods, this is supported by the reconstruction of intersections at railroad crossings. Introducing two level crossings through lowering or elevating the tracks should "allow both road and rail traffic to flow more smoothly and enhance safety."[46]

In Higashi-Kitazawa, approximately five kilometers west of Shinjuku, an improvement project is under way, which involves the reconstruction of both road and train infrastructure. While the privately operated Odakyu line completed the long planned relocation of the tracks and station underground in 2013, the city government is still in the process of reclaiming properties for a road-widening project. This expensive project—500 meters short and 10.3 billion yen (approx. US$99 million)—is part of the new auxiliary road 26. When completed, the road will link into a wider network that provides a continuous link from Tokyo Bay in the south, to Itabashi ward in the north. Currently, 1,950 meters of this link are under construction in multiple smaller segments. While some sections have already been completed and other segments are under construction, some parts are still in the planning process, because the road will cut through neighborhoods where no roads previously existed.[47]

The Highashi-Kitazawa segment involves the reconstruction of this small but incredibly busy neighborhood street into a road twenty to thirty-three meters wide, with two lanes and pedestrian sidewalks on either side. This represents a radical reconfiguration of the streetscape, where pedestrians and cars previously negotiated the space resulting in a much slower traffic speed. Wooden two-story buildings constructed right to the edge of the street will be replaced with multistory apartment blocks with ample setback from the street.

Overall, the width of the street profile will claim almost twice as much space as it had before. Not only will there be changes to the traffic flow and improvements to regional traffic-related issues, but the entire neighborhood character will also change along this section. The city government calls these additional works "improvement of urban landscape," a strategy that is seen as expanding the purpose of road infrastructure beyond pure efficiency. Carbon efficiency and a greener environment to "create an attractive cityscape"[48] are incorporated in road infrastructure projects and are seen as strategies to strengthen Tokyo's commercial competitiveness and attractiveness as an international tourist destination.

Whether these infrastructure projects deliver these larger aspirations is certainly debatable. Controversial projects—such as in Shimokitazawa, a trendy neighborhood popular among young Japanese and foreign tourists—demonstrate that the redevelopment of traffic infrastructure is not always in the interest of the wider community. Plans to relocate the two intersecting train lines underground and to begin construction of a municipal ring road in this small-scale neighborhood sparked massive community protests and international media attention. In addition, the multiplicity of individual plots, and more or less cooperative plot owners, involve a significant investment of time. For the northern segment of the Jujo project, the acquisition of land for the road extension is almost complete, leaving a wide strip of weirdly fenced-in land. The southern extension began in 2009 and is scheduled for completion in 2015. The project in Higashi-Kitazawa has a less ambitious schedule. Reconstruction began in 2006 and completion is not anticipated until 2025.

Land Subdivisions

Many smaller vacant lots often result from subdivision, which has had a dramatic effect on the urban fabric by supporting the fragmentation of urban plots. Yoshiharu Tsukamoto refers to this phenomenon as "subdivurban," a term that describes "patterns that emerge when a suburb is subdivided after being swallowed in a wave of urbanization."[49] This phenomenon is closely connected to taxation and planning policies, and significantly influenced the development of neighborhoods, particularly during the bubble economy. With inheritance tax rates up to 70 percent of the land value and skyrocketing land prices in the nineteen-eighties, subdividing land was often the only way to pay the outstanding taxes. While the current maximum tax rate of 50 percent is still regarded as high in Japan and may still be higher than in many other countries, inheritance tax only accounts for 3.4 percent of the total tax revenue.[50] Although the overall number of deaths has increased since the end of the bubble economy, the number of taxable cases has remained largely unchanged since early the 2000s.

A drastic drop in land prices since the beginning of the nineteen-nineties, as well as revisions made to the inheritance tax—including an increase in the basic exemptions[51]—reduced the number of cases that would fall under the highest tax bracket.

While this would suggest reduced financial burdens of the inheritance tax, the pressure is still high, largely due to the changing economic climate and the uncertain employment situation. General regulations further contribute to the financial pressure leading to vacancy of residential properties. As a rule, the inheritance tax in Japan "must be paid in one lump sum in cash."[52] Where the lump sum cash payment cannot be met, payment in kind (PIK)—for example, properties—are accepted. Currently, the property value is largely defined by the land price and empty land is taxed at a higher rate than land that has a residential structure on it. That means if a property is offered as a PIK, the inheritor has to clear the land and turn it into a vacant lot before it the property can go into the possession of the national government and be "put up for sale."[53]

The recent economic climate in Japan has encouraged the government to revise the inheritance tax again, this time to increase taxes, while also significantly reducing the basic deduction by 40 percent from the current figure.[54] While these major revisions were already planned for April 2011, they were delayed due to the Tohoku disaster[55] and are now scheduled to go in effect in January 2015. A few changes have already been introduced that address in particular the succession of small-scale land. For these properties, measuring between 200 and 240 square meters, the Japanese taxation system distinguishes whether or not the residence will continue to be occupied. While previous regulations allowed a reduction of up to 50 percent of the value of the land in cases where the successor decides to not to live in the property, the new conditions remove this option.

In the most recent revisions, the government further redefines small-scale residential land and now includes properties up to 330 square meters in this regulation. Given that the traditional multigenerational household is no longer the norm and that children are living separately from their parents with no intention of moving back into their parents' house, these revisions mean that many homes will remain vacant and "inheritors will be hit with higher taxes than before."[56]

Observing the interrelation between inheritance tax, subdivision, and vacancy in the past, it is very likely that these increasing financial burdens will have an impact on the production of small vacant spaces in the future. The rapidly aging population and large amount of homeownership among older generations will contribute to an increase in the number of inherited properties in near the future. For households with members sixty years old or older, around 70 percent own their dwellings. Furthermore, as Yosuke

Hirayama states, "owner-occupied housing, which used to be an effective means of producing capital gain, began to generate capital loss. Underlying the fall in house prices … there has been an over-construction of owner-occupied housing,"[57] resulting in cases where homeowners have become deeply indebted. Together with the decreasing birth rate and lower number of children, this will make it increasingly difficult for inheritors to pay their taxes.

Under these circumstances, subdividing land into even smaller lots seems to be the logical action. Yet, as the size of residential properties in Tokyo—already considered one of the smallest in the developed world—continue to shrink, we can question how sustainable further division of land is in the long run. What are the larger consequences of massive subdivision in Tokyo? And how much smaller can we divide land for residential purposes until the plots become unattractive for further development? Studying a neighborhood in Tokyo's Setagaya ward, Tsukamoto observed that the process of subdivision has reduced the average size of a residential plot to only 80 square meters, a third of the original 240 square meters measured in 1940.[58] Currently, it is not foreseeable what the minimum accepted land size would be for private residential property. In recent years, there has been an increase in newly built houses—even on lots as small as thirty square meters. The growing demand for these ultra-small homes demonstrates that in Japan, size is regarded as secondary and can be compromised when it comes to fulfilling the dream of individual homeownership.

Although the trend to subdivide is understandable on a personal level, particularly for individuals suffering from high inheritance taxes, the continuous reduction of land size comes at a price that affects the entire neighborhood. Outlining the consequences of subdivision on the neighborhood character, Tsukamoto identifies three generations of housing stock classified by distinct spatial characteristics.[59]

The first generation is defined as detached, single-story dwellings surrounded by private gardens and hedges, which contribute to a leafy and attractive neighborhood environment. The second generation is characterized by increased density, as taller buildings are constructed on smaller lot sizes. With further division of the land, the density constantly increases. In the third generation, the small and fragmented plots often result in strips, cul-de-sacs, or flagpole lot layouts. The latter is often the result of building regulations concerned with disaster mitigation and emergency access. These demand a two-meter street frontage for every newly constructed house. But these often weird-shaped spaces effectively become less attractive for residential development, because they require intelligent architectural design solutions. The newer housing generation is also constructed right to the limits of the property line.

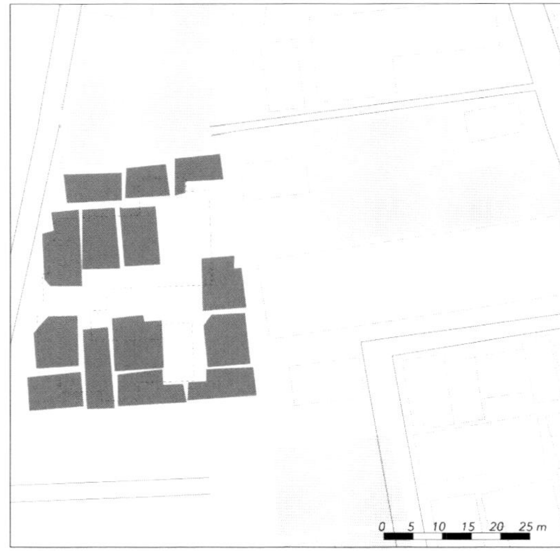

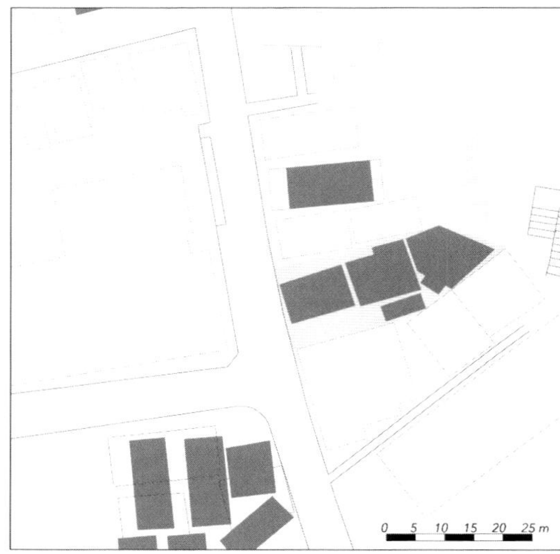

Subdivision: Examples in Itabashi-ku

Overlay of building footprints: Current new developments (dark grey), former buildings (red). The light grey areas demonstrate vacant plots.

Subdivision is an economic phenomenon largely related to inheritance and property taxes. The financial pressures will be felt more severely with an aging population, departure of traditional family patterns, and a declining number of inheritors, indirectly influencing vacancy.

Above: Transect showing the disparity of natural increase and decrease in population across the transect.

Below: Total fertility rate (TFR), aging population and decreasing household size across the transect (Based on TMG data in 2011)

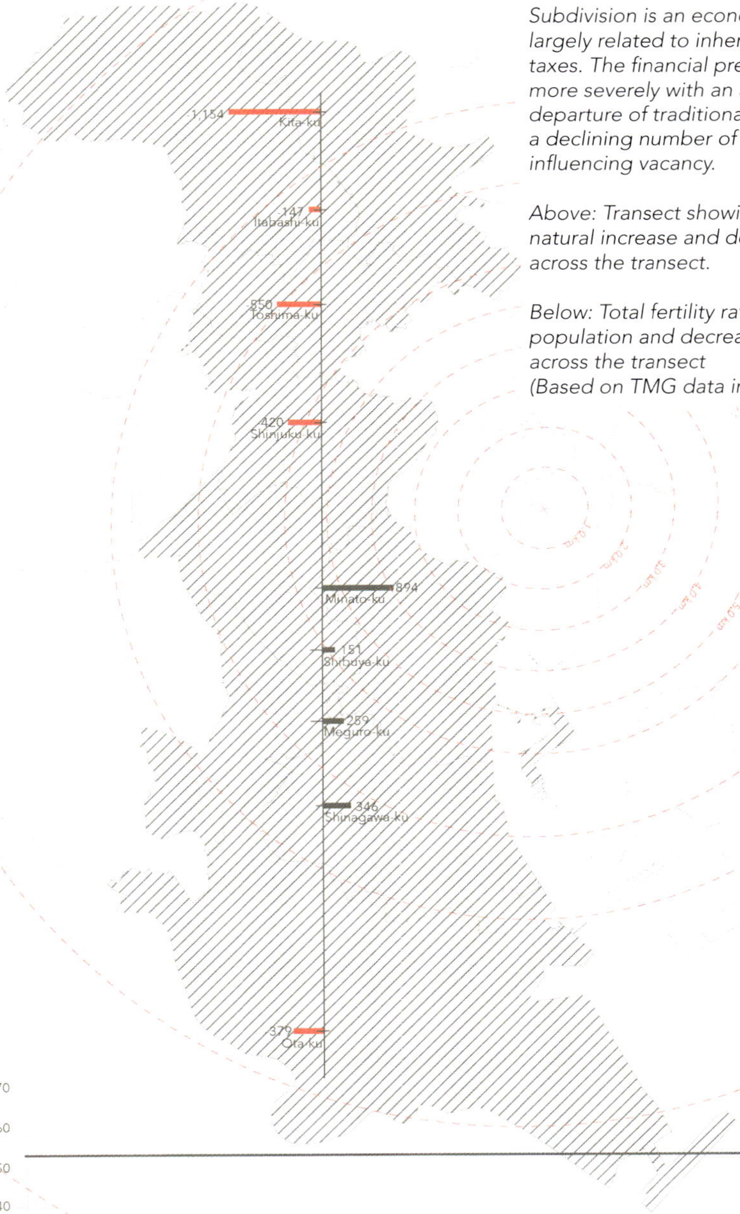

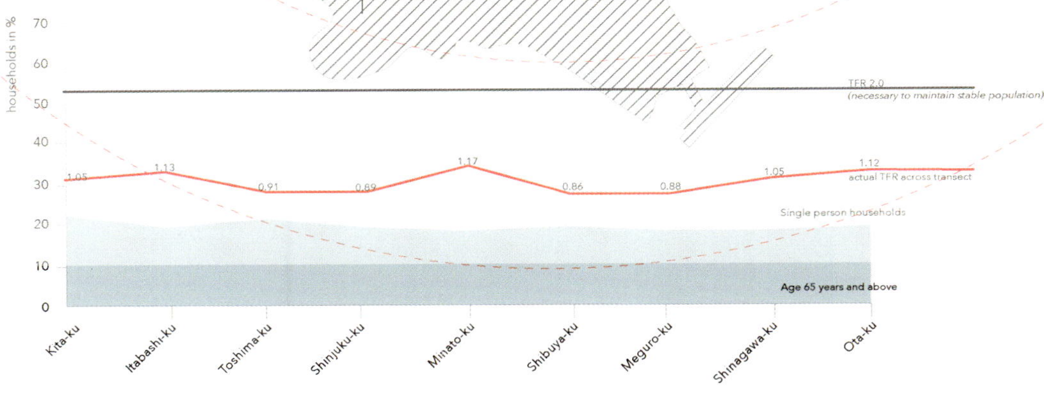

Lack of natural light, lack of privacy, and the demand for private car parking space are only a few challenges that result in an increasingly harsh delineation between the house and the street scene, which further separates the public and private realm.

Another consequence is the lack of greenery as the space to maintain even small gardens decreases with each generation of subdivision. Formerly attractive neighborhoods that were blessed with private gardens now face declining livability, because the loss of vegetation not only contributes to the visual character of the neighborhood, but also to the environmental qualities of the place—think mitigation of heat and air pollution. These circumstances prompted politicians and bureaucrats to reconsider planning policies relating to the issue of subdivision. As local governments start to put an end to shrinking lot sizes, it may in fact become increasingly challenging in the future to further subdivide land. For example, as one of the first wards to mitigate further fragmentation, Meguro ward introduced planning policies that restrict the lot sizes for a residence to a minimum of seventy square meters. This act can be understood as a measure to regulate declining neighborhood character and to maintain the livability by acknowledging the importance of greenery in dense residential areas.

CHAPTER 4

Time Flux

I'm actually quite different, but I don't get around to being it.

Ödön von Horvath[1]

Tokyo is a live laboratory in which we observe a wide range of conditions and effects of urban transformation, which occur simultaneously, at various speeds, and on large and small scales. Transformation processes are observed as an inherent part of the natural cycle of urban development tied in with economic and demographic trends, as discussed in detail in the previous chapter. Various factors contribute to urban transformation and we have seen that assumptions of "change as growth" have been challenged by "change as shrinkage and transformation." Unexpected states of change—including decline, catastrophic events, or stalled developments—operate at distinct speeds and patterns. Transformations over time express the contextualized nature of vacancy and relate individual sites to a larger scale.

Recording Urban Voids

Since 2009, we have mapped and revisited urban voids in yearly intervals in five case study areas in Tokyo.[2] Through a visual mapping process, we found that approximately 90 percent of the voids we have observed remain vacant for several years. Overall and on a smaller neighborhood level, the number of urban voids seems to remain remarkably stable. In this process of visual and GPS- and GIS-aided assessment, we found a challenging gap in acquiring the data: where voids occurred over a shorter period of time, less than a year, they simply were not recorded—neither in our, nonempirical cross section, nor by taxation status. What does this say about a method of recording something that is in an "in-between" state and at a scale of Tokyo?

Tokyo's urban land use statistics have included ***unused land*** since the 1984 census, and define it as: "Residential sites prior to construction, sites undergoing zone adjustment, demolished sites, deserted buildings and reclaimed lands." Prior to 1984, the statistics include the category ***wasteland***, which was defined as: "Uncultivated land with shrubberies, barren lands."

Speculative perforation

Tokyo's sprawling condition will continue to produce urban voids as replacements and intermediacies.

Land use data is gathered through land taxation records as of January 1 in each year surveyed.[3]

According to Tokyo's current (2014) land use statistics, the overall amount of unused land is 4 percent.[4] Over the past fifteen years, the amount of unused land in Tokyo has remained remarkably constant. Even during the bubble economy between 1985 (4.5 percent) and 1991 (6 percent)—when land prices where high and real estate considered an investment opportunity—similar amounts of vacant land existed in Tokyo. Furthermore, assumptions that the collapse of the economy in 1993 (4.1 percent) would lead to a spike in vacant land are incorrect. In fact, property owners chose to keep properties unoccupied and the vacancy of buildings increased. However, as discussed in Chapter Three, unused land is taxed at higher rates than occupied land, which is arguably the reason for higher building vacancies than unused land. The statistical data, based on taxation records, is nonspatial. The general figure of 4 percent vacant land for each of Tokyo's twenty-three wards remains abstract and at a distant scale. On closer observation, the fluctuation of vacancies becomes an important aspect. Through modern technology and tools such as Google Maps, it is possible to trace vacant spaces in an area over time. Depending on the interval in which data are recorded, this non-empirical method reveals the shifting of vacant land, which is not visible through an overall figure. While the overall quantity might remain similar, vacant spaces change on an individual level in the highly fragmented fabric of Tokyo, and reflect localized processes of growth, transformation, and decline. Similar to site observations and taxation records, the aerial images are limited in offering only specific moments in time. Yet, with a combined data set of photographs it becomes possible to trace individual sites over a period of time.

Speed and Pace of Change

Time is a fundamental principle incorporated in every development and transformation, but there is more detail to this than just the general notion of change. A critical aspect of time is the pace at which transformation processes happen, because this defines not only *whether* but also *how* we perceive the occurring changes. In other words, the recognition of the transformation processes seems to correlate with the scale at which vacant spaces occur. International case studies dealing with the phenomenon of vacancy over the last two decades are largely centered on the issue of the quantity of vacancies and their increase over time.[5] A shock is created by the perception of sudden change in a city—which seems prosperous at one moment, but is suddenly in transformation—and the number of vacant spaces rises. Yet, there is a clear image of what happens once the tipping point that creates a crisis arrives. The "broken windows theory," first described by sociologist James Wilson and criminologist George Kelling in 1982, explains the snowball effect of deterioration in nonmaintained spaces: "Broken windows lead to more broken windows. If no one fixes them, people take it as a sort of sign that breaking windows is tolerated. So they break more windows."[6]

Change patterns can be discussed by means of the speeds at which they occur. In some instances, the increase in vacancies occurs slowly, but at a regular, possibly predictable pace. The transformation processes follow what we may call "regular patterns" of urban transformation.

The negative effects of actions, such as suburbanization, may be unnoticeable in the beginning. Only after we see the dramatic level of vacancies in cities such as Philadelphia or many parts in Eastern Germany are the issues fully comprehendible and recognized.

In other areas, deindustrialization occurred at an accelerated speed, and unforeseen scale and pace. There, the decline of major industries affected smaller and related industries, creating an escalating snowball effect of decline. Changes in the built environment occurred rapidly, and issues were so complex and multilayered, that by the time political and planning representatives reacted with countermeasures to prevent further decline, it was too late (e.g., Detroit).

Planning and design intervention strategies discussed in these cases, largely focus on mitigating the impact of vacancies, by either considering the temporary activation of vacant spaces before these spaces are returned into a "productive" state or by accepting the fact that the "big holes the transformation processes left in many cities"[7] will never be filled again and actively "downsizing the city." Struggling to find a vocabulary that addresses this process, Selle argued in the early nineteen-nineties that cities could "grow backwards," and that urban shrinkage and decline were part of a natural process that needed distinct design and planning strategies and tools.[8]

Extreme and rapid changes that lead to the production of vacancies occur through destructive events like wars and natural disasters. One of the extreme examples is the impact of natural disasters: for example, Hurricane Katrina and the 2011 Great East Japan Earthquake and Tsunami, which, within hours devastated entire regions leaving behind barren land and full-scale destruction of the built fabric. Here, the scale and impact of the sudden change can mask or intensify preexisting issues of decline, and heighten the difficulty of rebuilding. Rebuilding efforts in Tohoku—devastated by the 3/11 earthquake disaster—are faced with having to "downsize," while maintaining momentum for economic performance. Here, another set of design tools and strategies is missing.

The Speed of Tokyo

Tokyo is one of the fastest cities in the world. Levine measured this through the time effectiveness of services—for instance, the time it takes to purchase a stamp at a local post office—and public transport punctuality.[9] Speed in this instance, however, should not be confused with hectic movements or stress. Tokyo is a city that flows efficiently. This is achieved by strict adherence to set rules and protocol. Subway trains arrive every two minutes, commuters line up in specifically marked areas, wait to let passengers alight, and then enter the train.

A normal stop for a commuter train transporting up to 2,000 passengers is one minute. The flow of pedestrians crossing the famous Shibuya crossing is stopped every two minutes, because everyone obeys the red traffic light.

Efficiency is one of the key priorities in the operation and construction of this city. Located on the waterfront of Tokyo's Chuo Ward, The Tokyo Towers, Japan's second tallest apartment buildings houses 8,000 people. The buildings were completed in 2008 after a construction period of precisely three years. The high speed of the construction—one floor every four days—was achieved by utilizing state-of-the-art technology, such as high-speed construction elevators.[10] This example illustrates an ideal of transformation in Tokyo; a city eager to be seen as high-tech driven, effective machine.

In Tokyo, buildings last twenty-six years on average.[11] Paul Waley positions Tokyo as a development-oriented city with few strategies in place concerning the historical legacy in the urban fabric. "Tokyo is an extreme case, a city founded some 400 years ago with very few substantial structures over 50 years old."[12] Thus, the legibility of Tokyo cannot be based on the individual building, but the composition of the fabric. Constant rebuilding does not promote any structural or spatial continuum that we are familiar with in most Western cities. In fact, Tokyo's entire urban fabric changes approximately every thirty-two years.[13]

Landscape elements largely form the few continuous aspects in this city. Even though rivers might be invisible and covered up by streets, street patterns reflect original positions. Historic terrace structures, embankments, moats, and walls remain elements that become reused in the city as railway corridors and building foundations. Parks and gardens have a stronger sense of continuity due to ownership structure and the policy-driven provision ratio for green and open space. Open spaces in the form of smaller public spaces engrave a plot size into neighborhood where the building footprints in the surrounding context constantly change. Where privately owned plots can be subdivided or merged to allow for more lucrative developments, urban parks, historic gardens remain somewhat of a constant.

However, the time frames of urban transformation projects are rather diverse and the pace of some redevelopment projects, particularly large-scale redevelopments, actually contradict this overarching agenda.

Tokyo's urban policy does not stipulate a process of forced acquisition to ensure a timely completion in large-scale redevelopment projects. This naturally leads to long-term interventions. Road readjustment projects are the obvious example. In general, it is difficult to predict how many years these projects require until they are completed. Some cases have proven that a single owner, reluctant to move or sell, can delay projects for an undetermined period of time. In Kjojima, for example, a dense and old neighborhood extremely vulnerable to the effects of earthquakes, a project was initiated in 1981 with the aim of widening roads. This contribution to disaster mitigation was planned on a 1,800-meter stretch of the road.

Fifteen years later, in 1996, only 186 meters of the initial plan had been achieved.[14] In these slow processes of readjustment, an aspect of small gaps shifts to a scene of decay, as more and more buildings disappear until only stoic individuals remain—but inevitably, they will also disappear.

Other projects on a similar scale, such as developer-driven redevelopments, may take the same amount of time. Highly dependent on the structure, vitality, and "attractiveness" of the neighborhood, some redevelopment projects may take a long time until completed.[15] For example, the Roppongi Hills development by Mori Corporation, took nearly seventeen years to acquire all the plots necessary for the eleven-hectare development complex in this centrally located and affluent part of the city. Much of that time was spent cutting through red tape and persuading hundreds of reluctant residents to move.[16] Smaller building projects in other parts of the city, such as in the working-class areas in Itabashi, take much less time—approximately thirteen months from the deconstruction of small dwellings to the completion of multiple high-rise condominium towers.

Where development is viable, voids will transform more quickly, as was discussed in the previous chapter. Short-term vacancies are observed in areas with higher economic vitality, and flexibility; yet this observation is contradicted by high rates of vacancies in Ginza, one example of an extremely affluent area. Upgrades to individual buildings and development processes depending on fewer owners tend to occur faster, as in the example of brownfield redevelopment sites. Slower processes shift parts of the urban fabric and the impacts of urban renewal will eventually be seen in the entire urban fabric. Two major trends can be seen currently: the traditional fine grain is exchanged with coarser grain of larger plots of housing and road infrastructure. Where once were narrow, walkable neighborhood streets are now roads with heavier traffic, lined by multistory apartment buildings that serve as fire breaks. A developer-driven market transforms entire blocks of small, detached houses in densely built neighborhoods into luxury high-rise condominiums towers, with ample private parking spaces included. In the other extreme, the subdivision of small plots continues to fragment the urban landscape.[17]

Redevelopment processes are slowed down significantly by complex factors, like ground contamination and the cost of larger plots on highly attractive land, as seen in Toyosu.

Fluctuating Vacancy

Yet while we consider change as naturally dynamic process, there are two related aspects that we want to focus on in regards to urban voids: the notion of a finished outcome and the scale with which we consider change. The vast scale of Tokyo challenges the idea of a finished outcome. Where a finished outcome of one element—a new building, block, or street—might be achieved, *other* parts of the urban fabric continue to change, as individual parts on similar or different scales. Where one vacant site is reprogrammed and a new building is finished, a site close by can become vacant at the same time. This simultaneous process produces a fluctuating pattern where an overall amount of vacant sites remains stable, but at the ground level, voids shift throughout an area and the city.

In the sense of Lefebvre, who considers urban spaces as mirror of a society's ambition and governing forces, Tokyo has to be considered a perpetually changing and adaptive organism that has grown out of society through culture and economic frameworks and demands. [18]

In a city in a constant state of flux, vacancies emerge as a logical by-product of the activities, maintaining a dynamic balance between appearance and disappearance. This balance is underlined by figures on vacant land that remain generally stable, but shift in close context and according to local conditions. As a consequence, the fluctuating condition produced by multiple voids calls for a consideration of a connected, dynamic network of spaces. This dynamic network challenges preconceptions of static forms and regulations by transcending legislative boundaries of ownership and administration, and reconnects a landscape system while posing complex questions in performative terms.

William Sherman discusses the disciplinary implications of this network understanding:

> Recasting the terms of boundary definition from the formal to the processive undermines oppositions such as the living and the inert, the ecological and technological, the dynamic and the static.... in this fluctuating territory, architects and landscape architects start to recognize that the world cannot simply be subjugated to human will.[19]

With this shift in understanding, time-based processes, and meta-systems of networked spaces in flux, new challenges for design in both disciplines are born. As a consequence of this condition, designers in both disciplines can no longer be passive; they need to become active agents in a multidirectional field.

New forms of collaboration—between formal and informal actors, disciplines and administrative agencies—lie at the core of this new intellectual setting. As Sherman further states: "Ways of thinking no longer constrained by historical assumptions about established boundaries between disciplinary or professional knowledge foster cultural invention."[20]

The field for this shift is clearly set in Tokyo's voids.

Urban Void, Shibuya, Shibuya-ku, 2009

Urban Void, Shibuya, Shibuya-ku, 2012

Urban Void, Yanaka, Bunkyo-ku, 2010

Right page top: 2011

Right page bottom: 2012

2009

2010

201

2009

2010

201

2009

2010

20

2009

2010

20

2009

2010

Recording Urban Voids: Motohasunuma, Kita-ku 2009–2012

2010

2012

2010

2012

Recording Urban Voids: Kirigaoka, Kita-ku 2010–2012

2009

2010

2011

2012

2013

Recording Urban Voids: Toyosu, Chuo-ku 2009–2013

EPILOG

Possibilities in Absence

We have discussed urban voids in Tokyo through performative and processual aspects. The shift between use and noninterference, large scale and detail, foregrounding materiality, and processes of becoming and change over time, suggesting readings as atmospheres and portraying types of uses, the incredible richness of Tokyo's voids becomes evident.

The main question—"how does the view on a familiar phenomenon change when considered in a new context?"—points to cultural readings that start to reframe the capacity of urban voids. Voids as empty spaces lack any definition of culture, yet they are situated in a specific context that has an impact on what they are and will become.

Now, we would like to expand on these aspects and unpack what we see as the possibilities in absence for Tokyo, and the definition of urban void in the discourse of landscape architecture. First, we start by outlining some of the contemporary conditions of society that we believe impact how public spaces are perceived and used. This, in turn, influences how urban voids can be seen as a possibility.

Through portioning void as a state of being in the world and pointing to the possibility of voids as catalysts for addressing the states of society, we aim to build a connection between the perspectives on void in a performative and hypothetical sense. In conclusion, we rephrase the key aspects in Tokyo that we see as possibilities in absence.

Void as Condition

Void can be considered as a field condition and metaphor for states of being. Tokyo Void suggests tying states of being together with physical states of becoming and forming, in an exploration of void as catalyst for the other, authentic, ephemeral states of being.

The 2008 film *Tokyo Sonata,*[1] mentioned in Chapter Three, portrays the contemporary paralysis and social alienation in Japanese society through the main protagonist, who has to cope with shame of losing social status through job loss, and who hides this loss from his family. Eventually, all of the family members in the film are trapped in isolation—unable to voice their fears and desires. This inability is not rooted solely in a contemporary situation of estrangement, but also in Japanese traditions of addressing shame and the divergence from normative roles.[2] The example of *Tokyo Sonata* is well suited to unpacking a problem that is bigger than Tokyo Void: the shift of societies in an age of social acceleration and their relation to public space.[3] This vast thematic can by no means be explored in this context, however, a few points resonate with the ideas of parks and relate to the question—"why are we drawn to urban voids?"

The emptiness and indifference of being in the world as described by Swiss-German philosopher Rahel Jaeggi is a condition of alienation where the world is apathetically perceived as something separate from our perceived self and a life as that ultimately is something foreign.[4] Jaeggi argues: the term alienation implies that an ideal unbroken, somehow organically grown identity exists somewhere within us. However, this paradox of the ideal self and its possibilities of becoming is problematic, as it implies that one was someone real before distancing oneself from the real. Social and political roles we use to construct and define our lives become triggers in the distancing and alienation of self. We assume roles, fulfill them, they give us meaning and define who we are. Rooted in social roles, we fulfill our lives without claiming them as us—because we often cannot. A paralyzing loss of a relation to one's own desires, ambitions, and experiences leads to the paradoxical incapability to integrate oneself into one's life experience.

Naturally, a question of transferability will arise here: are Japanese cultural concepts of group belonging similarly affected by this notion, which seems to speak to individuals? The point here is that roles might rarely be questioned, be they roles of individuals, groups, or spaces.

The expectations that are placed on specific experiences seem to be one main paradigm of how lives are perceived. We expect to grow in routines and any disturbance of the routine will be perceived as deep rupture. Urban spaces operate similarly. All programs work as a code to identify expectations. A park is something we expect to be a park.

Alarming trends of growing social isolation in Japan underline the issue of accelerated alienation: one-person households becoming the largest category among all household types for the first time in 2010[5]; dropping birth rates with lowest births on record in 2012; a staggering loss of interest in romantic relationships of 61 percent of men and 49 percent of woman aged eighteen to thirty-four stating in a 2011 survey that they were not interested in dating, let alone marriage.[6] These figures largely point to one of the highest gender imbalances among OECD nations: 70 percent of Japanese women leave their jobs after their first child due to long work hours, dim career prospects, and one of the biggest pay gaps between men and women in the OECD.[7] Breaking out of the mold of gender roles is made more difficult by economic decline, less job security, and minimal social welfare. Moreover, Japan is one of the largest and most rapidly aging societies worldwide, with economic instability, a record debt-to-GDP ration, social isolation, and natural disasters—all of which place the country in the challenging position of having to quickly develop progressive and effective strategies for a resilient future society. Yet, current political strategy seems to be deflected from the pressing issues.[8]

Being an accelerated, alienated society is not exclusive to Japan, but is a trend seen in a global context. Hartmut Rosa brings the temporal dimension to processes of modernization—such as differentiation, rationalization, and individualization—and describes a basic element of dynamization in the context of rigidity as a paradoxical complement of modern acceleration. In an accelerated society, the effects of technological advancements, leading to an acceleration in the pace of life, have consequences for identity and personality. Rosa sees the acceleration of social change as intrinsically linked to structural and cultural transformations of society. "The acceleration of cultural change in the form of comparatively faster and easier changes in lifestyles, fashions, leisure time practices, stocks of knowledge, familial, spatial, political and religious bonds and orientations thus constitutes one of the main traits of cultural modernization."[9] A consequence of acceleration that Rosa sees is the "urge to realize as many options as possible from the infinite palette of possibilities that life presents to us," in risk-free, consumer-oriented environments that sees the collective aim of "living life to the fullest." Further, Rosa states: "At the same time, this hunger for new things can never be satisfied: No matter how fast we become, the proportion of the experiences we have will continuously shrink in the face of those we missed."[10]

These positions resonate as particularly suited to a Western context with focus on individualized efficiency. However differently Japan might view its position in relation, the above mentioned conditions of isolation and alienation can affirm a similar late modern condition for Japan. Being isolated in technology-driven, accelerated experiences does not eliminate the desire and struggle to define a meaningful existence and self-realization, as demonstrated in the Tokyo Picnic Club's slogan "do your own picnic."[11]

Void as Canvas

We have discussed void as a metaphor for states of being. Now, we suggest considering possibilities for states of being in a context that might allow for authenticity, and considering void as catalyst for self-realization: urban voids.

Is the void ground providing for a shift of the void state?

In *Alienation*, Jaeggi describes tools that can be considered to reappropriate one's life: self-realization, autonomy, and authenticity.[12] Self-realization may be achieved through the way activities are conducted. In contrast to living a life that is perceived as automated drifting, autonomy offers the capacity to choose. Authenticity places a value on one's existence. What kind of space offers the reappropriation of one's life? In the philosophical context, the world may be considered a space for self-realization. In the practice of landscape architecture, it may be a more concrete space: urban spaces, non-programmed spaces, nonspaces. Void spaces?

Urban voids require ideas and imagination: they can become anything and they can change anytime. Their fleeting and uncertain existence sits close to our indeterminate and ephemeral existence. Intervening, making, testing, learning, requires tactile and experiential engagement; needs to feel and to understand, needs to assemble and to construct, needs to experience and to be. The examples discussed in Chapter One demonstrate that urban voids have the capacity to become catalysts for reappropriation, and generators of conscious states of being.

The decelerated immediacy of consciously being in a space in play—through exploration or making—adds meaning, fulfillment, and achievement even in a context accelerated through technology: there is something to tweet about when the rice is growing, the yurt is standing up. Urban voids contradict the expectations we place on a programmed, predictable urban environment that is ready for us 24/7. These spaces are attractive due to their unfinished and open-ended nature: voids offer active experience instead of passive consumption; voids bring us back to a possible urban nature—a nature that is immediate.

Voids for People

The people and the culture of everyday Tokyo demonstrate values of group-based consensus, careful negotiation of using a shared good—urban space—and the ingenuity to execute pragmatic ideas. We have observed that through individual action, ideas, and criticality, urban voids have become catalysts for social interaction and creative experiments. Void spaces are platforms and incubators that speak for the ideas they hold: allowing diversity and asking for engagement. Ondi is a gravel surface of fifty-three square meters, yet it has become a space so much richer due to the diverse and shifting nonprescribed programs that extend to the surrounding streetscape, evoking curiosity in passers-by and inviting participation to the action on-site. The immense capacity of a culture of respect and care for a shared environment is possibly the most striking asset for Tokyo. Could Tokyo's voids become a shared resource rather than individual properties?

A first step would be to make these spaces available. While there is great awareness of the boundaries and responsibilities that come with the physical and metaphysical demarcation of boundaries, Japanese culture sets up high thresholds that prevent engagement. On small scale, careful and considered negotiation takes place when informally encroaching on public territory with private flowerpot gardens. This practice forms a perfect example for individual action impacting on a larger group with a positive outcome in mind. Can this understanding be extended to urban voids? What may be successful examples are projects in which the communities—rather than individuals—are encouraged to participate. Community involvement is used in projects such as the greening of road infrastructure or the maintenance of public spaces, where neighborhood initiatives contribute to making parks useable by planting. Larger projects, such as the sea forest project Umi no Mori invite a wide range of activities beyond the planting and weeding, involving individuals, community groups, and schools.

A next step would be to consider agencies of public entities such as universities, high schools, or kindergartens—on the neighborhood level—and to incentivize creative engagement by groups or individuals. For this, municipal governments and community groups need to place the emphasis on reading the possibility of active engagement as positive, and not as nuisance. It is encouraging to see a response by municipal governments with regard to the practice of informal flowerpot gardens: technically illegal as they encroach on public streets and sidewalks, these gardens are nonetheless viewed positively by municipal governments. In a 2007 survey, Taito-ku ward officials stated that they regarded the informal gardens as part of Tokyo's greenery because: "It is simply the last individual green, such as gardens and green roofs, which can be considered."[13]

On the neighborhood level, ***machizukuri*** (town making)—a bottom-up participatory planning instrument—is in place and has been successfully used to design parks with public participation. Machizukuri is a uniquely Japanese planning instrument that is intrinsically based on culture and group processes, and has been vastly successful in what could be described as democratic urban design.[14]

NPO projects, such as Ondi and the Aoyama Farmers' Market and 246 Commons, demonstrate that small pop-up ventures can be successful and have a market in Tokyo. Alternative creative markets have been a long-time fixture in Tokyo's subculture, as Design Festa, Oedo Antique market, and Inokashira Park markets demonstrate. Even pop-up food stalls should be considered as tools to activate urban voids for social interaction. Commercialization of space through food culture has a long tradition in Japanese cities and will continue to play an important role in the framing of public space. Semi-informal mobile food stalls (*yatai*) and alleyway bars have long been established and enjoy popularity with a growing trend of outdoor activities and environmental awareness.

Agency by landscape architecture and urban design professionals can offer the management of larger areas, while considering performative aspects and socioeconomic conditions over time. Michio Tase,[15] a prominent landscape architect and inventor renowned for groundbreaking and resource-minimizing planting strategies, provides a great example of taking agency for a socioeconomic system: in his off-campus project, Tase has initiated the subsidization of train tickets for students in Tokyo whose homes are in the rapidly depopulating northern Japanese prefectures. By allowing students to travel home frequently, he argues, ties with local communities are maintained and students are less likely to migrate to Tokyo upon graduation to find work. This strategic initiative emphasizes the capacity of landscape architects to think laterally in systems on multiple levels in time-based processes to assess impacts on a socioeconomic and environmental level. Considering this professional capacity for Tokyo's voids, a vast array of possibilities can emerge.

However, whether informal practices and citizen participation will be considered an alternative practice to actively shape urban planning and design, as seen in Berlin[16] remains questionable. While the Tokyo Metropolitan Government (TMG) frequently produces ambitious plans to increase the amount of Tokyo's urban green space, the qualitative aspects of urban green spaces remain fully neglected in these schemes.[17] A shift from quantitative aspects to qualitative aspects, foregrounding the capacity of citizens, should occur to make effective changes. What urban voids offer is multiplicity: flexibility to accommodate a range of programs, Tokyo's voids should be considered in multiple terms. As discussed, programmatic performance can be viewed active and passively—and in the passive sense, the spaces should be utilized to address Tokyo's vulnerability. Despite countless predictions, it is only a matter of *when* a major earthquake will strike Tokyo. Scenarios include vast destruction caused by seismic shock, fire, and flooding. Considering urban voids as infrastructure to mitigate large-scale disasters would allow expanding the repertoire of strategic tools. Even if we speculate that in an aftermath of a large-scale earthquake urban voids would be appropriated and used as evacuation bases, would it not be timely to consider them in this capacity before a disaster? To deregulate and to simplify, to incentivize and to let established cultural norms of mutual respect and civic engagement play out, putting Tokyo's people first, has already started to change Tokyo, and building on this momentum will transform Tokyo entirely.

Void as Continuous Landscape

Tokyo's urban voids offer a tremendous capacity to contribute to the sustainable urban regeneration of Tokyo. Four percent of Tokyo's land area is space that could function as microhabitats, buffers for urban heat islands, and mitigation of other extreme climate events. A network of small, dispersed, yet interconnected spaces can fulfill all eco-functions of green spaces—such as the provision of open soil in an otherwise fully sealed urban context, rainwater runoff collection, biodiversity, dust absorption, and improvement of the microclimate. In the context of Tokyo, the urban wilderness, on a micro scale, truly renders the perspective of the Other.

In this continuous landscape system, vegetation is a palimpsest of interference and noninterference, a live laboratory of plants in Tokyo. This capacity is astounding and should be considered a powerful tool to read Tokyo as an ecosystem. In abstracting the notion of ecology and using this in considering urban systems, it will be possible to uncover layer upon layer of diverse and connected environmental entities. Even small and dispersed spaces are connected by climatic conditions, water flows, and topography. The anthropocentric view of delineated artificial boundaries has distanced us from the continuous landscape that we inhabit. Tokyo's voids can teach us to rediscover this nature by helping us seeing their depth and capacity.

Voids can be read as individual and dispersed entities, and also as networks of spaces that continuously shift and change as they grow and decay, regrow. Herclitus's "everything is in flux" describes best the condition that permeates our lives. Yet, it is interesting to observe that the systems we inhabit and use are designed to deny change, and a strong urge to identify outcomes as fixed entities directs all processes. Striking examples of Japanese gardens meticulously designed and maintained to be perfect and virtually stand still come to mind. Here is a major challenge: to see diversity and change and to accept both as intrinsic to all processes and systems.

Ephemerality is deeply engrained in Japanese culture, but not technology. It seems as if a reminder is timely to extend the embracing of change and questioning of the fixed notions of modernity to a dynamic urban context. Seeing Tokyo as an ecosystem requires repositioning notions of nature as something "out there" to "everything around us." Tsukamoto describes Tokyo as "complex intertwining of people, the flow of things, elements of the environments and time." He goes on to suggest: "If we observe the micro eco-systems as cross-categorical adjacencies … we can have plenty of fun, rather than being weighed down by the solemnity of a single building."[18]

Tokyo defies classification. Urban voids should not be exempt from this, but be included in the micro eco-systems of irrational delight.

Outlook

Tokyo has a tremendous possibility to change the world's view on Asian megacities, through celebrating and fostering innovative practices by its citizens. In the context of shrinking populations and outdated models of consumption, Tokyo can lead the way to understanding the capacity of a dynamic hybrid urbanism, which is shaped by citizens through engagement, and by governments through opening the possibilities for this to occur. That way, new typologies for public spaces and engagement grow from old models.

The contribution that a closer understanding of Tokyo's voids can bring to a theoretical discourse on urban voids and urban transformation is a truly distinct perspective rooted in the culture and specifics of the context. The question of whether landscape architecture and urban design should solely be seen as a beautifying amenity creator will arise from this context.

Possibilities in absence are rich and manifold; shifting the view to allow new ideas to emerge is the main task.

Emptiness accommodates everything. I wonder if thoughts of all kinds intrude themselves at will on our minds because we call our minds vacant? If our minds were occupied, surely so many things would not enter them.

Yoshida Kenkō[19]

Notes

Preface

1 Julian Worrall and Erez Golani Solomon, *21st Century Tokyo: A Guide to Contemporary Architecture* (Tokyo: Kodansha International, 2010).
2 Roji Suzuki, "Tokio—Stadt Der Luecken / Tokyo—City of Gaps," *Arch*+, no. 151 (2000): 22–23.
3 Anuradha Mathur and Dilip Da Cunha, *Deccan Traverses: The Making of Bangalore's Terrain* (New Delhi: Rupa, 2006), ii.
4 Ibid.
5 See Sanki Ichikawa's introduction to the English translation of Kenko's *Essays in Idleness* dated June 25, 1914. In Kenko, *Essays in Idleness: The Tsurezuregusa of Kenko* 2nd ed., trans. Donald Keene (New York: Columbia University Press, 1998).

Introduction: Voids in Density

1 Stalker Collective, see "Stalker through the Actual Territories," http://digilander.libero.it/stalkerlab/tarkowsky/manifesto/manifesting.htm
2 Momoyo Kajima, Junzo Kuroda, and Yoshiharu Tsukamoto, *Made in Tokyo* (Tokyo: Kajima, 2008).
3 Atelier Bow-Wow and Tokyo Institute of Technology Tsukamoto Architectural Lab, *Pet Architecture Guide Book* Vol. 2, Living Spheres (Tokyo: World Photo Press, 2001).
4 Tokyo Metropolitan Government, *Tokyo Statistical Yearbook* (Tokyo: Tokyo Metropolitan Government Bureau Of General Affairs Statistics Division Management and Coordination Section, 2010).
5 Senatsverwaltung für Stadtentwicklung Berlin, Referat Freiraumplanung und Stadtgrün, "Öffentliche Grünflächen in Berlin," 2010.
6 Department of City Planning City of New York, "2010 Primary Land Use: Each Borough's Lot Area by Land Use Type," 2010.
7 Hiroshi Ota, "Thinking Your Own Public Space: The Ten Years of Tokyo Picnic Club" in *Exposure,* ed. Marieluise Jonas and Rosalea Monacella (Melbourne: Melbourne Books, 2012), 199–208.
8 Jared Braiterman, "Tokyo's Urban Design Role," *The Japan Times,* Nov 27, 2009, http://www.japantimes.co.jp/opinion/2009/11/27/commentary/tokyos-urban-design-role
9 See Hajime Ishikawa, "The Landscape Book: A Look at the Ground," *Contemporary Architect's Concept Series* 12 (2012).
10 Ignasi De Solà-Morales Rubio, "Terrain Vague," in *Anyplace,* ed. Cynthia Davidson (Cambridge, MA: MIT Press, 1995), 118–23.
11 Ibid., 120.
12 Carl Cassegard, "The Atelier and the Park," *The World (And Books)* (blog), July 23, 2010, http://carlcassegard.blogspot.de/2010/07/atelier-and-park.html
13 Philipp Oswalt, ed., *Shrinking Cities—Volume 1: International Research,* on behalf of the German Federal Cultural Foundation (Ostfildern-Ruit: Hatje Cantz, 2005).
14 Alan Berger, *Drosscape: Wasting Land in Urban America* (New York: Princeton Architectural Press, 2006).
15 See Heidi Müller, Gisela Schmidt, and Klaus Selle, "Stadtentwicklung Rückwärts! Brachen als Chance? Aufgaben, Strategien, Projekte," *AGB-PT-Bericht* 52 (2003); Klaus Overmeyer, ed., *Urban Pioneers*, ed. Senatsverwaltung für Stadtentwicklung. (Berlin: Jovis Verlag, 2007).
16 Overmeyer, *Urban Pioneers*.
17 See Gilles Clément, "Working with (and Never against) Nature," in *Environ(Ne) Ment: Approaches for Tomorrow,* ed. Giovanna Borasi (Milan: Skira, 2006), 90–104; Anna Jorgensen and Richard Keenan, ed., *Urban Wildscapes* (London: Routledge, 2012).
18 Cited in Cassegard, "The Atelier and the Park," 12.

19 Kenya Hara, *Shiro [White]*, trans. Jooyeon Rhee (Tokyo: Chuokoron-Shinsha, 2008), 45.
20 Yoshida Kenkō, *Essays in Idleness: The Tsurezuregusa of Kenko* 2nd ed., trans. Donald Keene (New York: Columbia University Press, 1998).
21 Darko Radovic, *Another Tokyo: Places and Practices of Urban Resistance* (Tokyo: Ichii Shobu, 2008), 32.
22 Christoph Brumann and Evelyn Schulz, ed., *Urban Spaces in Japan* (London: Routledge, 2012), 2.
23 Berger, *Drosscape*.
24 Paul Waley, "Re-Scripting the City: Tokyo from Ugly Duckling to Cool Cat," *Japan Forum* 18, no. 3 (2006): 363.

PART ONE: The Performance of Tokyo's Vacant Space

1 Antoine Picon, "Anxious Landscapes: From the Ruin to Rust," *Grey Room* 01 (Fall 2000): 64–83.
2 James Hamblin, "Our Unhealthy Fear of Vacant Land," *The Atlantic,* December 14, 2012, http://www.theatlantic.com/health/archive/2012/12/our-unhealthy-fear-of-vacant-land/266188
3 Ibid.
4 Luc Lévesque, "The 'Terrain Vague' as Material—Some Observations," http://www.amarrages.com/textes_terrain.html
5 See John Brinckerhoff Jackson, *Discovering the Vernacular Landscape* (New Haven: Yale University Press, 1986); Elizabeth Meyer, "Sustaining Beauty: The Performance of Appearance. A Manifesto in Three Parts," *Journal of Landscape Architecture* 3, no. 1 (2008): 6–23.

Chapter 1: Intervention, Transgression, and Appropriation

1 Since 2009, the Tokyo Void research project, undertaken by the authors, documents vacant space in Tokyo and forms the basis for this book. (www.tokyovoid.com)
2 Jared Braiterman, "Ginza Rice Farm," *Tokyo Green Space* (blog), July 15, 2009, http://tokyogreenspace.com/2009/07/15/ginza-rice-farm/.
3 See Philip Brasor and Masako Tsubuku, "The Rise and Fall of Property Taxes," *The Japan Times*, January 3, 2012, http://www.japantimes.co.jp/community/2012/01/03/how-tos/the-rise-and-fall-of-property-taxes/
4 See Luc Lévesque, "The 'Terrain Vague' as Material—Some Observations," http://www.amarrages.com/textes_terrain.html; David Gissen, *Subnatures: Architecture's Other Environments* (New York: Princeton Architectural Press, 2009).
5 Gissen, *Subnatures*.
6 Gordon Kanki Knight, "Fab 40: The Sea Forest, Tokyo Bay," *Wallpaper* Magazine Fab 40: Japan,* October 14, 2009, http://www.wallpaper.com/architecture/fab-40-the-sea-forest-tokyo-bay/3834.
7 Tokyo Metropolitan Government, "Umi No Mori (Sea Forest)," (Tokyo: Marine Parks Section, Waterfront Development Division, Bureau of Port and Harbor, 2008).
8 Edan Corkill, "Icon and Iconoclast," *The Japan Times*, December 7, 2008.
9 Ando, quoted in Yuka Sano, "Why Does Ando Plant Trees?" *Casa Brutus*, 2009: 106–7.
10 *Tokyo Sonata,* directed by Kiyoshi Kurosawa (Tokyo: Fortissimo, 2008), DVD
11 See works by Hidenobu Jinnai, *Tokyo: A Spatial Anthropology* (Berkeley: University of California Press, 1995); and Christian Dimmer, "Re-Imagining Public Space: The Vicissitudes of Japan's Privately Owned Public Spaces," in *Urban Spaces in Japan: Cultural and Social Perspectives,* ed. Christoph Brumann and Evelyn Schulz (London: Routledge, 2012), 74–105.
12 Heike Rahmann, "Small Is Beautiful," (PhD diss., The University of Tokyo, 2008).
13 In a 2003 paper on homeless people in Japan, Kakita outlines the different definitions regarding homelessness. While European studies clearly distinguish between "homeless

people" and "rough-sleepers," in Japan, "the term 'homeless people' refers exclusively to 'rough sleepers.'" Homeless people in Japan are almost exclusively male (95.2 percent) and the majority lives in the two biggest cities. Yusuke Kakita, "Homeless People in Japan: Characteristics, Processes and Policy Responses," *The Annals of Sociological Association, Osaka City University* 5 (2004): 7–20.

14 Ministry of Health, Labor and Welfare and Ministry of Land, Infrastructure and Transport. "Hōmuresu no jiritsu no shien-tō ni kansuru kihon hōshin (Basic Policy on Support of the Independence of Homeless)," 2013. According to this report, the number of homeless people dropped by 62 percent compared to the first national survey on the state of homeless people in 2003, when more then 40 percent of the surveyed people indicated they were living in public parks. Ministry of Health, Labor and Welfare. "Hōmuresu No Jittai Ni Kansuru Zenkoku Chōsa Hōkoku-Sho No Gaiyō (Overview of National Survey Report on the State of Homeless People)," 2003. The study is available online at http://www.mhlw.go.jp/houdou/2003/03/h0326-5.html

15 For more discussion on this topic, see Marieluise Jonas, "Private Use of Public Open Space in Tokyo. A Study on the Hybrid Landscape of Tokyo's Informal Gardens," *JoLA Journal of Landscape Architecture*, no.4 (November 2007): 18–29; Marieluise Jonas, "Hybrid Landscapes of Tokyo's Informal Gardens—Case Study Yanaka," in *Another Tokyo—Places and Practices of Urban Resistance,* ed. Darko Radovic (Tokyo: ichii shobou, 2008).

16 André Sorensen, "Shrinking Cities and Liveablity in Japan: Emerging Relationships and Challenges," in *Urban Spaces in Japan: Cultural and Social Perspectives,* ed. Christoph Brumann and Evelyn Schulz (London: Routledge, 2012), 212.

17 "Coin Camping Tents24," http://www.mi-ri.com/tents24/about.html

18 Lévesque, "The 'Terrain Vague' as Material."

19 Ophuis further suggests: "We have to interpret the park new to our cultural needs of our times.... Perhaps the park of the future is closer than we are willing to admit. And do we not complete its image in our heads?" Hans Ophuis, "Brauchen wir noch Parks? Do we still need Parks?" *Topos—The International Review of Landscape Architecture and Urban Design* (2002): 74–79.

20 Tokyo Picnic Club official website, *http://www. picnicclub.org*

21 246 Common official website, http://246common.jp

22 Wildmagic Urban Outdoor Park official website, http://wildmagic.jp/

23 "Wild Magic," *Tokyo, Time Out,* http://www.timeout.jp/en/tokyo/venue/12648/Wild-Magic.

24 Japan's first official farmers' market began in 2009 in eight cities across the country under the catchy French name "Marche Japon." This movement aims to promote farmers' markets and local produce in Japanese cities. The initiative is supported by the Ministry of Agriculture, Forestry and Fisheries as part of the Food Action Nippon initiative. For more information, see http://www.marche-japon.org (Japanese). Food Action Nippon is a government initiative to increase food self-sufficiency. Japan's heavy reliance on food imports, declining agricultural business, and the massive production of food waste cause serious problems in Japan, pushing the government to increase general awareness about food production, distribution, consumption, and sustainability. See http://syokuryo.jp/fan/ for more information (Japanese).

Chapter 2: Matter & Materiality

1 Atelier Bow-Wow, *Made in Tokyo* (Tokyo: Kajima Institute, 2001).

2 Fumihiko Maki, *Nurturing Dreams: Collected Essays on Architecture and the City* (Cambridge: MIT Press, 2008).

3 Ibid.

4 Donald Ritchie, "Ein Spaziergang Durch Tokio / A Walk through Tokyo," *Arch+*, no. 151 (2000): 58–63.

5 Thomas Daniell, *After the Crash: Architecture in Post-Bubble Japan* (New York: Princeton Architectural Press, 2008), 165.

6 Alison Margaret Smithson and Peter Smithson, *The Charged Void: Architecture* (New York: Monacelli, 2001).
7 David Gissen, *Subnatures: Architecture's Other Environments* (New York: Princeton Architectural Press, 2009), 142.
8 Tokyo land use statistics 2011: approximately 6 percent of Tokyo's urban areas are parks, 4 percent unused land and waste land, and 1 percent farm land. There are no statistics describing the composition and distribution of different types of surface material.
9 Susumu Yasuda, et.al, "Characteristics of Liquefaction in Tokyo Bay Area by the 2011 Great East Japan Earthquake," *Soils and Foundations* 52, no. 5 (2012): 793–810.
10 Tokyo Gas, "Agreements on Land Sale and Purchase and the Cost-Sharing for Measures Against Soil Contamination of the Toyosu District Site," (2011).
11 NHK, "Toyosu Shin Ichiba No Kensetsu-Hi Ga Kōtō (Construction Costs of New Toyosu Market Soaring)," *NHK Online* (2013). Published electronically Dec 27, 2013, http://www3.nhk.or.jp/news/html/20131227/k10014165901000.html. (accessed December, 29, 2013)
12 Market, Metropolitan Central Wholesale, "Toyosu Shin Ichiba Kensetsu Ni Tsuite (About the Construction of the Toyosu New Market)," http://www.shijou.metro.tokyo.jp/index.html. Detailed info on findings of toxic material is also accessible through:
http://www.tokyoichiba-project.metro.tokyo.jp/measures/index.html
Further information on the progress of the decontamination works can be accessed online:
http://www.toyosusinsijyo-kouji.jp/progress/
13 See Jun Hongo, "Plan to Move Venerable Tsukiji Market Draws Fire," *The Japan Times,* Aug 24, 2007, http://www.japantimes.co.jp/news/2007/08/24/news/plan-to-move-venerable-tsukiji-market-draws-fire/#.UvcLgvb40he; David Cyranoski,
"Missing Data Spark Fears over Land Clean-Up," *Nature,* April 26, 2010, http://www.nature.com/news/2010/100426/full/news.2010.199.html.
14 Chris Cooper and Katsuyo Kuwako, "Tokyo Fails to Find Builders for World's Biggest Fish Market," *Bloomberg News*, Nov 19, 2013, http://www.bloomberg.com/news/2013-11-19/tokyo-fails-to-find-builders-for-world-s-biggest-fish-market.html.
15 Hidenobu Jinnai, *Tokyo: A Spatial Anthropology,* (Berkeley: University of California Press, 1995).
16 Hajime Ishikawa, *The Landscape Book: A Look at the Ground,* Contemporary Architect's Concept Series 12 (Tokyo: LIXIL Publishing, 2012).
17 Ibid.
18 Hermann Hesse, *The Glass Bead Game,* (Harmondsworth: Penguin, 1972).
19 Ignasi De Solà-Morales Rubio, "Terrain Vague," in *Anyplace,* ed. Cynthia Davidson (Cambridge, MA: MIT Press, 1995), 118–23.
20 James Hamblin, "Our Unhealthy Fear of Vacant Land," *The Atlantic Monthly,* December 14, 2012, http://www.theatlantic.com/health/archive/2012/12/our-unhealthy-fear-of-vacant-land/266188.
21 De Solà-Morales Rubio, "Terrain Vague."
22 Gissen, *Subnatures.*
23 Tokyo Metropolitan Government Bureau of the Environment, "Guidelines for Heat Island Control Measures" (2005).
24 Gissen, *Subnatures.*
25 Atelier Bow-Wow and Tokyo Institute of Technology Tsukamoto Architectural Lab, *Pet Architecture Guide Book,* Living Spheres Vol. 2 (Tokyo: World Photo Press, 2001).
26 Momoyo Kajima, Junzo Kuroda, and Yoshiharu Tsukamoto, *Made in Tokyo,* (Tokyo: Kajima, 2008).
27 See Paul Waley, "Moving the Margins of Tokyo," *Urban Studies* 39, no. 9 (2002): 1533–50; Y. Ashihara, *The Hidden Order: Tokyo through the Twentieth Century,* (Tokyo & New York: Kodanshita International, 1989); Hidenobu Jinnai, *Tokyo: A Spatial Anthropology*.
28 Hajime Ishikawa, *The Landscape Book: A Look at the Ground.*
29 Gilles Clément, "Working with (and Never against) Nature," in *Environ(Ne)Ment: Approaches for Tomorrow,* ed. Giovanna Borasi (Milan: Skira, 2006), 90–104.
30 Eric Sanderson, *Mannahatta: A Natural History of New York City,* (New York: Abrams, 2009).

PART TWO: Tokyo's Spatial Capital

1 See Alan Berger, *Drosscape: Wasting Land in Urban America* (New York: Princeton Architectural Press, 2006); Wendy Knight, "A Waterfront That Has Left Its Wasteland Days Behind," *The New York Times,* Mar. 7, 2007; Julie Slabinski, "Comment: From Wasteland to Oasis: How Pennsylvania Can Appropriate Vacant Urban Land into Functional Space Via Urban Farming," *Widener Law Journal* 22, no. 253 (2012).
2 Luc Lévesque, "The 'Terrain Vague' as Material: Some Observations," http://www.amarrages.com/textes_terrain.html
3 Berger, *Drosscape*, 236.
4 Ibid., 237.
5 Lévesque "The 'Terrain Vague' as Material," http://www.amarrages.com/textes_terrain.html
6 Ibid.
7 Anna Jorgensen and Richard Keenan, ed., *Urban Wildscapes* (London: Routledge, 2012).
8 Ignasi De Solà-Morales Rubio, "Terrain Vague," in *Anyplace,* ed. Cynthia Davidson (Cambridge, MA: MIT Press, 1995), 118–23, here 110.
9 Barrie Shelton, *Learning from the Japanese City: Looking East in Urban Design* Vol. 2 (London: Routledge, 2012), 129.
10 Berger, *Drosscape,* 236.

Chapter 3: The Politics of Vacancy

1 Tokyo Metropolitan Government, *Tokyo Statistical Yearbook* (Tokyo: Tokyo Metropolitan Government Bureau Of General Affairs Statistic Division Management and Coordination Section, 2011).
2 Ibid.
3 W. R. Garside, *Japan's Great Stagnation Forging Ahead, Falling Behind* (Cheltenham: Elgar, 2012), 168.
4 Martin Fackler, "Japan's New Optimism Has Name: Abenomics," *The New York Times,* May 20, 2013 http://www.nytimes.com/2013/05/21/world/asia/hope-in-japan-that-abenomics-may-be-turning-things-around.html?pagewanted=all&_r=0
5 Junichiro Okata and Akito Murayama, "Tokyo's Urban Growth, Urban Form and Sustainability," in *Megacities: Urban Form, Governance, and Sustainability*, ed. André Sorensen and Junichiro Okata (Tokyo: Springer, 2010), 15–41.
6 Christoph Brumann and Evelyn Schulz, ed., *Urban Spaces in Japan: Cultural and Social Perspectives* (London: Routledge, 2012), 8.
7 Tokyo Metropolitan Government, *Tokyo Statistical Yearbook.*
8 National Institute of Population and Social Security Research in Japan (IPSS), "Population Projections for Japan (January 2012): 2011 to 2060." The complete report can be accessed at http://www.ipss.go.jp/index-e.asp
9 Kyodo, "Japan's Fertility Rate Logs 16-Year High, Hitting 1.41," *The Japan Times*, June 6, 2013 http://www.japantimes.co.jp/news/2013/06/06/national/japans-fertility-rate-logs-16-year-high-hitting-1-41/
10 IPSS, "Population Projections for Japan (January 2012): 2011 to 2060."
11 Editorial, "Vacant Houses Pose a Problem," *The Japan Times-Opinion*, Sep 6, 2013. http://www.japantimes.co.jp/opinion/2013/09/06/editorials/vacant-houses-pose-a-problem/#.U4q8kC9MoaA
12 IPSS, "Selected Demographic Indicators for Japan," http://www.ipss.go.jp/p-info/e/S_D_I/Indip.asp#t_25.
13 André Sorensen, "Shrinking Cities and Liveablity in Japan: Emerging Relationships and Challenges," in *Urban Spaces in Japan: Cultural and Social Perspectives*, ed. Brumann and Schulz.
14 Ibid.
15 Brumann and Schulz, ed., *Urban Spaces in Japan*, 8.

16 Hidetoshi Ohno, "Fiber City: Tokyo 2050," http://www.fibercity2050.net/eng/fibercityENG.html.
17 Brumann and Schulz, ed., *Urban Spaces in Japan,* 8
18 IPSS, "Selected Demographic Indicators for Japan"
19 Julian Ryall, "Tokyo Population to Halve in Next 90 Years," *Telegraph*, Sep 4, 2012. http://www.telegraph.co.uk/news/worldnews/asia/japan/9519203/Tokyo-population-to-halve-in-next-90-years.html
20 Volker Elis and Ralph Lützer, "Regionalentwicklung Und Ungleichheit: Raumdisparitäten Als Thema Zur Prime Time—Eine Einführung," in *Regionalentwicklung Und Regionale Disparitäten (Japanstudien 20)*, ed. Volker Elis and Ralph Lützer (Munich: Ludicium, 2008), 15–33.
21 Tony McNicol, "Home Sweet Danchi," *Highlighting Japan* (February 2008): 28–29.
22 Philip Brasor and Masako Tsubuku, "Danchi Housing Lets You Think Outside the Usual Box," *The Japan Times*, November 11, 2012.
23 National Tax Agency, "National Tax Agency Report 2012," (Tokyo: National Tax Agency, 2012).
24 Philip Brasor and Masako Tsubuku, "Don't Judge a House by Its Exterior," *The Japan Times*, March 6, 2012. http://www.japantimes.co.jp/community/2012/03/06/how-tos/dont-judge-a-house-by-its-exterior/#.U4q87i9MoaA
25 Ministry of Land, Infrastructure, Transport and Tourism, "Trends Concerning Land in Fy2011" (2012).
26 Sorensen, "Shrinking Cities and Liveablity in Japan," 210.
27 Ibid.
28 Ministry of Land, Infrastructure, Transport and Tourism, "Trends Concerning Land in FY2011."
29 Sorensen, "Shrinking Cities and Liveablity in Japan," 212.
30 Minoru Mori, "Cultivating the Vertical Garden," in *Reimagining Japan: A Quest for a Future That Works*, ed. McKinsey & Company (San Francisco: VIZ Media, 2011), 417–22.
31 McCormack, p. 59.
32 Tetsuo Seguchi and Patrick Malone, "Tokyo: Waterfront Development and Social Needs," in *City, Capital and Water*, ed. Patrick Malone (London: Routledge, 2006), 164–94, here 164.
33 Ibid.
34 Julian Worrall and Erez Golani Solomon, *21st Century Tokyo: A Guide to Contemporary Architecture* (Tokyo: Kodansha International, 2010), 46.
35 Roman Cybriwsky, *Tokyo: The Shogun's City at the Twenty-First Century* (Chichester: Wiley, 1998).
36 Seguchi and Malone, "Tokyo," 171.
37 Tokyo Metropolitan Government, Bureau of Port and Harbor, http://www.kouwan.metro.tokyo.jp/.
38 Alan Berger, *Drosscape: Wasting Land in Urban America* (New York: Princeton Architectural Press, 2006), 51.
39 André Sorensen, "Land Readjustment and Metropolitan Growth: An Examination of Suburban Land Development and Urban Sprawl in the Tokyo Metropolitan Area," *Progress in Planning* 53 (2000): 219.
40 Hiroko Tabuchi, "After Quake, Japanese Choose Peace of Mind over Great View," *The New York Times*, July 19, 2011. http://www.nytimes.com/2011/07/20/business/global/in-tokyo-high-rise-apartment-sales-plunge.html?pagewanted=all
41 Paul Waley, "Who Cares About the Past in Today's Tokyo?" in *Urban Spaces in Japan: Cultural and Social Perspectives*, ed. Brumann and Schulz.
42 Foreign Press Center Japan, "Tokyo Super Eco Town Press Tour," http://fpcj.jp/en/assistance-en/tours_notice-en/p=8959/.
43 Tokyo Metropolitan Government, Bureau of Urban Development, "Urban Development in Tokyo" (Tokyo: Tokyo Metropolitan Government, 2011).
44 Source: Tokyo Metropolitan Government, Bureau of Environment, "Traffic Volume and Traffic Speed in Tokyo." http://www.kankyo.metro.tokyo.jp/en/data/

45 Tokyo Metropolitan Government, Bureau of Construction, "Road Construction," http://www.kensetsu.metro.tokyo.jp/english/douro/gaiyo/01.html.
46 Ibid.
47 Ibid.
48 Tokyo Metropolitan Government, Bureau of Urban Development, "Urban Development in Tokyo," (Tokyo: Tokyo Metropolitan Government, 2011).
49 Yoshiharu Tsukamoto, "Escaping the Spiral of Intolerance: Fourth-Generation Houses and Void Metabolism," in *Tokyo Matabolizing*, ed. Koh Kitayama, Yoshiharu Tsukamoto, and Ryue Nishizawa (Tokyo: Toto, 2010), 28–44.
50 National Tax Agency, "National Tax Agency Report 2012."
51 Ministry of Finance, "Let's Learn More About Taxes" (Tokyo: Ministry of Finance online brochure 2013). http://www.mof.go.jp/english/tax_policy/publication/tax005/index.htm
52 Ernst &Young, "International Estate and Inheritance Tax Guide 2013" (Online brochure).
53 Abe Naobumi and Michael Brase, *The Complete Guide to Japanese Systems* (Tokyo: IBC, 2012).
54 Ministry of Finance, "Let's Learn More About Taxes."
55 Japan Property Central, "Revisions to Inheritance Tax in Japan," http://japanpropertycentral.com/.
56 Ibid.
57 Yosuke Hirayama, "The Changing Context of Home Ownership in Japan," (Report Kyoto University (2004) :2. http://www.housingauthority.gov.hk/hdw/ihc/pdf/hayh.pdf
58 Yoshiharu Tsukamoto, "Escaping the Spiral of Intolerance."
59 Ibid.

Chapter 4: Time Flux

1 The original quote in German: "Eigentlich bin ich ganz anders, nur komme ich nicht dazu." (Translated by author)
2 Tokyo Void is an Internet platform that was designed by Marieluise Jonas and Heike Rahmann in 2009 to link vacant sites with potential users utilizing mobile technology, such as QR-coded tags and GPS data. GPS data of 180 temporary vacant sites were recoded on a Google Map that is linked to the website. The bilingual website attracted mainly academics and students, primarily foreign residents of Tokyo, who were looking for spaces to use. The main problem the project faced was obtaining contact and ownership details of sites and owners, in order to facilitate connections between users and providers. A 2009 and 2010 QR-code tagging project failed to draw attention to the spaces. However, the 2010 site installation "space ambassador," at the Ondi site, brought public attention to the project—not as designed (utilizing mobile and web technology), but through public response and engagement of a Sunday crowd. http://www.tokyovoid.com
3 Tokyo's Land use statistics are published in the annual *Tokyo Statistical Yearbook*. The yearbook compiles comprehensive statistical data for Tokyo-to, including population, economic, and environmental data. For more information see http://www.toukei.metro.tokyo.jp/tnenkan/tn-eindex.htm
4 Tokyo Metropolitan Government, Tokyo, Tokyo Statistical Yearbook, http://www.toukei.metro.tokyo.jp/tnenkan/tn-eindex.htm. The website, updated January 22, 2014, contains data from 2011, land use are dated 2006–2007
5 See Philipp Oswalt, *Shrinking Cities: Volume 1 International Research* on behalf of the German Federal Cultural Foundation (Ostfildern-Ruit: Hatje Cantz, 2005); Karina Pallagst, Thorsten Wiechmann, and Cristina Martinez-Fernandez, ed., *Shrinking Cities: International Perspectives and Policy Implications* (Oxford: Routledge, 2010); Marcel Langner, and Wilfried Endlicher, *Shrinking Cities: Effects on Urban Ecology and Challenges for Urban Development* (New York: Peter Lang Publishing, 2007).
6 James Hamblin, "Our Unhealthy Fear of Vacant Land," *The Atlantic Monthly,* December 14, 2012, http://www.theatlantic.com/health/archive/2012/12/our-unhealthy-fear-of-vacant-land/266188.

7 Alan Berger, *Drosscape: Wasting Land in Urban America* (New York: Princeton Architectural Press, 2007), 346.
8 Heidi Mueller, ed., *Stadtentwicklung Rueckwaerts!—Brachen Als Chance?: Aufgaben, Strategien, Projekte: Eine Textsammlung Für Praxis Und Studium* (Dortmund: Dortmunder Vertrieb für Bau- und Planungsliteratur, 2003).
9 The examples of speed are taken from Robert Levine, *Eine Landkarte Der Zeit: Wie Kulturen Mit Zeit Umgehen* (Munich: Piper, 2003). General aspects of time and representation are taken from Daniel Rosenberg and Anthony Grafton, *Cartographies of Time: A History of the Timeline* (New York: Princeton Architectural Press, 2013).
10 Marieluise Jonas, "I Love New Tokyo. Questioning Contemporary Urban Identities of Tokyo and Their Potential for Sustainable Urban Regeneration," *Weimarpolis Multidisciplinary Journal of Urban Practice* 1, no. 2 (2009).
11 Atelier BOW-WOW, *Bow-Wow from Post Bubble City,* (Tokyo: INAX, 2006).
12 Paul Waley, "Who cares about the past in today's Tokyo?" in *Urban Spaces in Japan: Cultural and Social Perspectives,* ed. Christoph Brumann and Evelyn Schulz (Oxford: Routledge, 2012), 148.
13 Hiroshi Ota and Shuichi Matsumura, *Understanding Tokyo,* ed. Global Center of Excellence for Sustainable Urban Regeneration. Vol. 2 (Tokyo: Center for Sustainable Urban Regeneration, The University of Tokyo, 2005).
14 Hohn, *Stadtplanung in Japan* p. 369 ff.
15 André Soerensen, *The Making of Urban Japan Cities and Planning from Edo to the Twenty-First Century* 1st ed. (London: The Nissan Institute / Routledge Japanese Studies series, 2002).
16 Martin Fackler, "The Builder Who Pushes Tokyo into the Clouds," *The New York Times*, March 27, 2008, http://www.nytimes.com/2008/03/27/business/worldbusiness/27mori.html?scp=1&sq=The%20Builder%20Who%20Pushes%20Tokyo%20Into%20the%20Clouds&st=cse (accessed January 21, 2011).
17 Atelier BOW WOW, *Bow-Wow from Post Bubble City*.
18 "The spatial practice of a society secretes that society's space" in Henri Lefebvre, Henri, *The Production of Space,* trans. Donald Nicholson-Smith (Oxford: Blackwell, 1991 [1974]), 38.
19 William Sherman, "Engaging the Fields, Fields in Flux," in *Site Matters*, ed. Carol Burns and Andrea Kahn: (New York/Oxford: Routledge, 2005), 312.
20 Ibid., 314.

Epilog: Possibilities in Absence

1 *Tokyo Sonata,* directed by Kiyoshi Kurosawa (2008).
2 Discussion of guilt in context of World War II points out distinct culturally based understandings and perceptions of guilt and shame in Japan and Germany. See Ian Buruma, *The Wages of Guilt: Memories of War in Germany and Japan* (London: Atlantic Books, Limited, 2009).
3 Hartmut Rosa and Jonathan Trejo-Mathys, *Social Acceleration: A New Theory of Modernity* (New York: Columbia University Press, 2013).
4 See Rahel Jaeggi, "Aneignung Braucht Fremdheit," *Texte zur Kunst*, no. 46 (2005); Rahel Jaeggi, *Entfremdung Zur Aktualität Eines Sozialphilosophischen Problems,* Frankfurter Beiträge Zur Soziologie Und Sozialphilosophie Vol. 8, ed. Axel Honneth (Frankfurt/New York: Campus Verlag, 2005).
5 "Single-Person Households Forecast to Jump to 37% in 2035: Report," *The Japan Times,* January 20, 2013, http://www.japantimes.co.jp/news/2013/01/20/national/single-person-households-forecast-to-jump-to-37-in-2035-report/#.UvgrVvaCNgK.
6 Abigail Haworth, "Why Have Young People in Japan Stopped Having Sex?" *The Guardian,* October 20, 2013, http://www.theguardian.com/world/2013/oct/20/young-people-japan-stopped-having-sex
7 Rupert Wingfield-Hayes, "Japan: The Worst Developed Country for Working Mothers?" March 22, 2013, http://www.bbc.co.uk/news/magazine-21880124.

8 "NHK Governors Back Abe Agenda, Minutes Reveal," *The Japan Times,* February 9, 2014, http://www.japantimes.co.jp/news/2014/02/09/national/nhk-governors-back-abe-agenda-minutes-reveal/#.UvgupfaCNgI.
9 Rosa and Trejo-Mathys, *Social Acceleration* p. 281.
10 Hartmut Rosa, "Do More, Faster: The Consequences of Accelerated Modern Life," July 4, 2013, http://www.spiegel.de/international/zeitgeist/hartmut-rosa-essay-acceleration-plagues-modern-society-a-909465.html.
11 Tokyo Picnic Club (TPC) was founded in 2002 to celebrate the bicentennial anniversary of picnics, which became popular through the activities of the "Pic-Nic Club" founded in London in March 1802. Over eighty people with various professional backgrounds—e.g., architect, urban designer, landscape designer, graphic designer, illustrator, photographer, food coordinator, editor, curator, etc.—are members of TPC. Members dedicate their creative talents to redefining the activities of picnic in the modern context of urban Tokyo; activities that range from developing sandwich menus and tea flavors, to renovating the park management systems and its landscape qualities. To criticize the narrowness of public spaces and their exclusive management, TPC is claiming the "Picnic Right," as a basic human right for the urban dwellers of Tokyo. For more information, visit http://www.picnicclub.org/english/aboutus.html.
12 Rahel Jaeggi, *Alienation* (New York: Columbia University Press, 2009).
13 Marieluise Jonas, "Private Use of Public Open Space in Tokyo. A Study on the Hybrid Landscape of Tokyo's Informal Gardens," *JoLA Journal of Landscape Architecture,* no. 4 (November 2007): 18–29; See Marieluise Jonas, "Potscape. A Study on the Hybrid Landscape of Tokyo's Informal Gardens" (PhD diss., The University of Tokyo, 2008).
14 Machizukuri has been widely discussed in: Uta Hohn, *Stadtplanung in Japan Geschichte-Recht-Praxis-Theorie* 1. ed. (Dortmund: Dortmunder Vertrieb für Bau- und Planungsliteratur, 2000); Andre Soerensen, *The Making of Urban Japan Cities and Planning from Edo to the Twenty-First Century,* 1st ed. (London: The Nissan Institute / Routledge Japanese Studies series, 2002). Recently, critics have pointed out, however, that machizukuri has become a placard term used by government agencies to mask a top-down planning process. See: Neil Evans, "Machizukuri as a New Paradigm in Japanese Urban Planning: Reality or Myth?" *Japan Forum* 14, no. 3 (2010): 443–64.
15 Michio Tase, landscape architect, ecologist, and inventor runs Plamtago—a one-man landscape architecture practice in Tokyo. Notable projects include: ACROS FUKUOKA (Nihon Sekkei, Inc., Takenaka Corp., Tase Michio Plamtago) and Queens Meadow Country House, Tono. Tase describes his work as "Passive Architecture & Active Landscape with Nature." In an interview with Jared Braiterman of TokyoGreenspace Blog, which can be found at:
http://tokyogreenspace.com/2009/05/21/meeting-tase-michio-%E7%94%B0%E7%80%AC%E7%90%86%E5%A4%AB/)
16 Philipp Oswalt, Klaus Overmeyer, and Philipp Misselwitz, *Urban Catalyst: The Power of Temporary Use* (Berlin: DOM Publishers, 2013).
17 Tokyo Metropolitan Government, "2012 Action Program for Tokyo Vision 2020," http://www.metro.tokyo.jp/ENGLISH/PROFILE/policy03.htm. The Tokyo Green Plan 2012 is available as a PDF download at: http://www.kankyo.metro.tokyo.jp/en/greenery/biodiversity.html
18 Tsukamoto, *Made in Tokyo* p. 36.
19 Yoshida Kenkō, *Essays in Idleness: The Tsurezuregusa of Kenko* 2nd ed., trans. Donald Keene (New York: Columbia University Press, 1998).